"I recall he told me in detail about the H.H. Holmes ca
That was a particularly cruel and long-undetected mas
of the century. I don't know where Fish read about it."
- Dr. Fredric Wertham

"Why, he was such a gentle sort of man. You wouldn't think he would step on an
insect. He was so kind and fatherly. How he fooled us!"
- Mrs. Delia Budd

"There could have not been a kinder father. I do not understand what could have possessed
him in the circumstances revealed by this trial. Of course, he was out of his proper mind."
- Gertrude DeMarco, Fish's Daughter

"Asked whether the presence of the needles in Fish's body would result in any complications when the current is applied in the electric chair. Warden Lawes said: 'If Fish is
electrocuted and the needles are in him, the flesh around the needles would probably
be burned. The shock is so sudden, however, that he never would know it. We hav-
en't ever considered the possibility of complications when the current is turned on.' "
- New York Daily Mirror, March 30, 1935

"That skunk would do anything. Frequently he used to undress in front of small children and once some one found him nude in his bedroom beating himself with a whip.
Up to a couple of months ago I worked with him in an apartment house at 1883 Am-
sterdam Ave., Manhattan. I did all the work and he collected all the money. He used
to wake up often in the middle of the night, screaming. Usually it was something like:
'Bud! Bud!' Naturally, I didn't connect it at the time. He quit after the tenants got up a
petition against him. There were half a dozen complaints that he had abused children."
- Albert Fish Jr.

"I do remember him, although I was only five. I was playing by the candy store, while Mummie stood by the baby carriage. He came up and took
hold of my hand. I was frightened because he was such a bent old man…He
asked me if I was alone…and I told him, no, that my mother was over there…
then he looked at her, and I pulled my hand away and ran back to Mummie."
-Mary Little

ALBERT FISH IN HIS OWN WORDS

The Shocking Confessions of the Child Killing Cannibal

Edited by John Borowski

Waterfront Productions

ALBERT FISH IN HIS OWN WORDS

Transcription of Fish's Handwriting by Lauren Kalal

Published by:
Waterfront Productions
P.O. Box 607085
Chicago, IL 60660
U.S.A.

ISBN
978-0-692-26375-4

SEE THE ALBERT FISH FILM!

A FEATURE DOCUDRAMA FILM BY FILMMAKER JOHN BOROWSKI.

"One of the most disturbing films that I've seen"- Kitley's Krypt

"Riveting and unsettling" - Videoscope Magazine

albertfishfilm.com

CHICAGO WORLD'S FAIR SERIAL KILLER!
SEE THE FILM! READ THE BOOK!

hhholmesthefilm.com

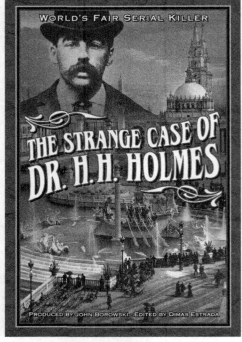

strangecase.com

OTHER FILMS BY FILMMAKER JOHN BOROWSKI

serialkillerculture.com

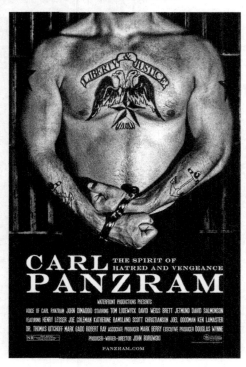

panzram.com

BOY OF 7 STRANGLED IN WOOD NEAR HOME

His Suspenders Used by Assailant to Put Policeman's Son to Death.

STATEN ISLAND IS AROUSED

Sixty Detectives Seeking Man Seen Walking Near the Lad Before the Murder.

CONTENTS

THE PERVERSIONS (PARAPHILIAS) OF ALBERT FISH
(From Dr. Wertham's Files)

Sadism: The infliction of pain and bodily injury for sexual satisfaction.

Masochism: Having others inflict pain on oneself in order to obtain sexual pleasure.

Active and passive flagellation: Whipping and being whipped.

Self-castration and castration: The cutting off of one's own genitals or those of another.

Exhibitionism: Showing oneself in the nude, Usually done when standing in the window.

Voyeur acts: Peeping and looking at others who are either nude or who perform sexual acts.

Piqueur acts: Sticking needles into others or into oneself for sexual motives.

Paedophilia: Sexual acts with children.

Homosexuality: Sexual relations with one's own sex.

Penilinctio: Application of mouth to penis.

Fellatio: Same as penilinctio.

Cunnilingus: Application of mouth to female genitals.

Anilingus: Application of mouth to rectum.

Coprophagia: Eating of feces.

Undinism: Playing with urine; for example, urination into another person's mouth.

Fetishism: Abnormal preference for one part of the body, such as buttocks, or for inanimate objects.

Cannibalism: The eating of human flesh.

Hyperotism (or hyperhedonism): Abnormal intensity of the sexual instinct.

INTRODUCTION
By Filmmaker John Borowski

In 2007, my feature docudrama film based on the life of Albert Fish (Albert Fish: In Sin He Found Salvation) was released on DVD in North America. I still feel that Fish's life and crimes are the most disturbing, yet fascinating, of all true crime cases in history. In 2010 I was delighted to discover that the Library of Congress opened all 222 containers of Dr. Fredric Wertham's research files to public research access. It was Dr. Wertham who examined Fish and testified for the defense at Fish's trail in March of 1935. Dr. Wertham's files are not only important as an insight into the demented mind of Albert Fish, but they are also important becuase they draw attention to the gaping holes in the American justice system where authorities fail to apprehend criminals, but then the criminals are given vengeful punishments when they are finally apprehended. When the laws of society fail the public, THEN they feel they have the right to execute people and pass sentences. I found it interesting that Fish was in the hands of authorities, including New York's Bellevue psychiatric hospital, numerous times and he fooled them all! Fish wasn't highly intelligent, but he was very cunning. If an unassuming old man could con the New York city police department and prominent psychiatric institutions, then how can our United States of America presume they can guarantee the safety of our own American citizens from others like Albert Fish? The world is inundated with true life cases of parental and relative abuses on children that have gone on far too long for no one to notice and these often result in physical and psychological trauma for the children and sometimes death. Why can't the system prevent these crimes from occurring? Modern crime fighting techniques are blown out of proportions on television shows. Multi-murderers have been labeled as serial killers by the U.S. government, hoping to prove to the public that the national murder epidemic can be magically cured by "profiling" these criminals. Yet, the murder rate rises and so does the frequency of especially brutal and tortuous murders. Workplace and school mass murders also continue to rise without an end in sight as we continually condemn the murderers, but fail to focus on the reasons why the murderers planned their attacks. I agree with Fish's attorney James Dempsey when he asks: "Do we have to wait until a madman like Fish commits one of the murders that we know he has been planning in his distorted mind for almost fifty years?" In the end, society wanted revenge, their pound of flesh, for Fish's murdering Grace Budd. Instead, Fish should have been placed in a psychiatric institution, as Jeffrey Dahmer should have been. But the press labels serial killers as monsters, giving the public the impression they are salivating creatures. Fish was a father, grandfather, and human being. The only regret I have in the making of my first film (H.H. Holmes: America's First Serial Killer) is that I called serial killer H.H. Holmes a "monster".We must not forget that these serial killers and criminals are still human beings and should be treated as such, even in their sentencing by the courts.

"The verdict in the case of Albert H. Fish proves nothing else but that we are still burning witches." - James Dempsey, Fish's Defense Attorney

Albert Fish (Mugshot)

PART I

MASKS HAVE NO EARS

FROM *THE SHOW OF VIOLENCE* (1949)

Fredric Wertham, M.D.

Fredric Wertham was a psychiatrist who studied in London, Erlangen, Munich, Würzburg, Paris, and Vienna. Following graduation from medical school in 1922, Wertham worked briefly at the Kraepelin Clinic in Munich under Emil Kraepelin, who developed the standard system for the classification of mental disorders. Later that year Wertham immigrated to the United States, where he accepted a position under Adolf Meyer at the Phipps Psychiatric Clinic at Johns Hopkins University. In 1926 Wertham published his first book in collaboration with Florence Hesketh, a biology instructor and sculptress, whom he married the next year. In 1932 they moved to New York, where Wertham was appointed senior psychiatrist at Bellevue Mental Hygiene Clinic. For the remainder of his professional career, Wertham lived in New York and was affiliated with numerous psychiatric organizations. In 1935 he testified for the defense in the trial of Albert Fish, declaring him insane. In addition to his medical activities, he was a prolific writer and public speaker. In particular, he issued constant warnings about the harmful influence of violence in the mass media. In the late 1970s, Wertham and his wife retired to Bluehills, their country home in Kempton, Pennsylvania, where he died in 1981. Included in the papers are correspondence, research notes, writings, newspaper and magazine clippings, memoranda, reports, patient case files, transcripts of court proceedings, psychiatric tests, drawings, photographs, miscellaneous biographical information, and other materials pertaining to Wertham's work and to the history of psychiatry during his lifetime.

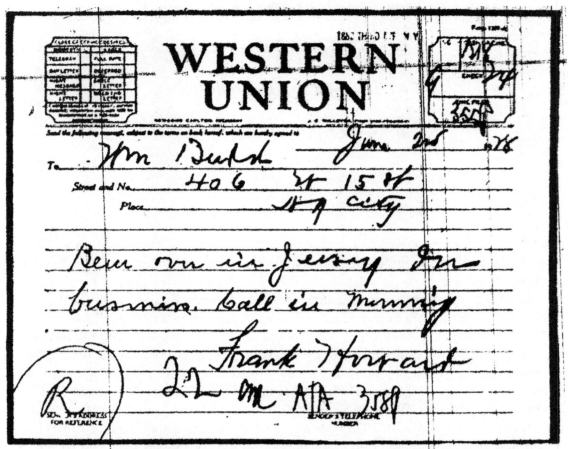

This telegram, signed Frank Howard, was sent to the Budds just before Grace disappeared with him.

Silence settled over the courtroom. "May it please your honor…" The district attorney was getting up ponderously to open his case. From the back row where I was sitting I could see only his new haircut and his thick neck. He cleared his throat and surveyed the jury.

"May it please the court, Mr. Foreman and gentlemen of the jury. This defendant is charged with murder in the first degree, in that he choked to death one Grace Budd in the town of Greenburgh in this county.

"In 1928, the People will prove, there lived down in the city of New York the Budd family. There was the father Albert, the mother Delia; there was Grace, there was Edward. Edward Budd was looking for a job. And so he put an ad in the newspaper that read in substance: 'Youth 18 wishes position in country.'

"In a day or so this defendant appeared at the Budd home. He said his name was Frank Howard, that he had seen the ad in the newspaper, that he had come to see Edward about the job. He said that he had a farm located down in Farmingdale, Long Island, a truck farm, and wanted to know if Edward could work on it. He also said he was married but had not been living with his wife. He was the father of six children. He said he had this truck farm and raised vegetables.

"Grace was a young girl at that time, approximately ten years and nine months of age. While he was sitting there the defendant said to the Budd parents that his sister was giving a party, a birthday party for her children, and he thought it would be nice if Grace would go along with him to that party. He said he loved children, he would return early that night, they need not worry. They hesitated to let her go but finally consented that Grace should go with him.

"So she left home, that little flat, on Sunday afternoon shortly after the noon hour with this defendant, and her parents have never seen or heard from her since.

"A report was made the next day to the police station that Grace had gone away and had not returned. The police department assigned a detective to this case and an investigation was made into her whereabouts.

"During the intervening years, from 1928 to the fall of 1934, clues were traced down by the police.

"On or about the eleventh day of November 1934, a letter was received at the Budd apartment. This letter was written by the defendant. It was unsigned. It was addressed to Mrs. Delia Budd.

"The letter, in substance, says that a friend of his by the name of Captain John Davis shipped from San Francisco for Hong Kong, China. It was dangerous for boys and girls under the age of twelve years to be at large out on the street because they would be seized and cut up and their meat sold. This man, Cat=ptain Davis, on arriving back at the city of New York, seized two boys, one eleven and one six, and he took the boys to his apartment and he stripped them. Locked them in the closet, and used to beat them up, and finally he killed the boy eleven an he ate his meat. Finally he killed the boy six and fried and stewed and parboiled his meat and ate him. 'And so I came,' says the letter, 'to your flat on the third day of June, 1928, and under the pretense of taking your daughter Grace to a party at my sister's I took her up to Westchester County, Worthington, to an empty house upt here, and I choked her to death. I cut her up and ate a part of her flesh. I did not have,' said the letter—I will use the word 'connection' with

7

her instead of the word used in the letter. She died a virgin. The letter was unsigned. But in that letter appeared an address, and on the back of that envelope in which this letter came was a symbol having in it the letters of a benevolent association in New York.

"Now the detective got that letter and he followed it through. He finally found that this defendant lived down on Fifty-second Street in the city of New York. After waiting for him for a considerable period of time he finally arrested him on the thirteenth day of December.

"At police headquarters this defendant stated that on the third day of June, 1928, he left his bundle in which was a cleaver—a butcher's cleaver—a knife, and a saw at a newspaper stand on the corner before going to the Budd flat. After he had taken Grace under his pretense of going to his sister's children's birthday party, he picked up this bundle which consisted of tools wrapped in canvas, then he took the elevated and finally took the New York Central to the town of Greenburgh. Grace was with him at the time. He got off the train and made his way to what is commonly known as Wisteria Cottage, He says that he took her in the room and choked her to death, and that it took about five minutes to do it. He knew that she was dead. Then he says he took her clothes off and cut her head off. Then he cut her across the body above the navel, he says, and left the lower part of her body and the torso behind the back door in the room. He took the head out to the outdoor toilet in back of the house and covered it over with a paper. Three or four days later he says he came back to this particular house and took the various parts of her body, three in number, and threw them over the stone wall which is at the back of the house.

"Now after making this statement the defendant took the New York police up to Worthington, took them up to the stone wall where he left this body in three parts. And, after searching around at the place where he said he left the body, the police found certain bones. It is the contention of the People in this case that those are the bones of Grace Budd.

"Now, in the first instance in this case there is a presumption of sanity. This defendant is legally sane. But he is sexually abnormal. His acts were abnormal, but when he took this girl from her home on the third day of June, 1928, in doing that act and in procuring the tools with which he killed her, bringing her up here to Westchester County, and taking her up to this empty house surrounded by woods in the back of it, he knew it was wrong to do that, and he is legally sane and responsible for his acts.

"That is a brief resume of what the People will prove in this case."

Throughout the district attorney's address everyone in the courtroom listened, fascinated—the judge, the jurors, the audience, the eighteen or twenty reporters at the big press table set up in the front of the courtroom. The defendant. Mr. Fish, small, gray, and indifferent, drowsed unconcernedly in his chair with his head resting on one hand.

As I listened I thought back over the whole case, my connection with it and the first time I had ever seen Albert Fish.

Six years ago little Grace Budd, aged ten, had disappeared. Then her mother had received this incredibly cruel letter. Fish's arrest followed eventually from the clue of the imperfectly inked-out return address on the envelope that had contained his letter. He confessed immediately (six times) and guided the authorities to the secluded house where, in the place he pointed out, the bones were uncovered.

The first time I saw him, he was in jail. He looked like a meek and innocuous little old man, gentle and benevolent, friendly and polite. If you wanted someone to entrust your children to, he would be the one you would choose. Many people who came into contact with Fish during the trial made that comment about him.

At first he regarded my visit as a routine matter of not much concern to him. He wrote to his daughter: "Some doctor came and asked me 1,000,000 questions." But when he realized that I was really scientifically interested, was probing into details and going to check them, was determined to understand him really, his detachment changed to interest. The whole procedure of examination took a long time and a number of sessions. He showed a certain desire to make himself understood and even to try to understand himself. The last time I saw him he said quietly: "I'll never forget you, Doctor."

He told me that he was concerned bout his children, and his face lit up for the first time when he spoke about his first grandchild. "She's twelve years old and in 7-A. She's a great little dancer. I just idolize her. She's going to take up stage dancing. I love children and was always soft hearted. Murder was not in my heart at all. It never was."

His attitude toward his immediate situation was one of almost complete detachment. "I have no particular desire to live. I have no particular desire to be killed. It is a matter of indifference to me. I do not think I am altogether right."

"Do you mean to say that you are insane?"

"Not exactly. I compare myself a great deal to Harry Thaw in his ways and actions and desires. I never could understand myself."

Somewhat incongruously, however, he expressed indignation about the fact that he was also charged with kidnapping. He explained to me that "both parents gave their permission. The mother objected at first to the party. But Grace's father said, 'She doesn't see much good times anyway. Let her go. She's always cooped up in this dark cellar.' Then the mother agreed too."

Fish also complained about the prisoner who had the cell next to him. "The cell I am in is nice and light, but I can't stand that man cursing all the time. I can't read my Bible. Religion was always one of my strong points, and I don't smoke, drink, or chew. I always had on my mind the last three years that I had to confess. I realized that I'd never be able to do what I originally intended—carry the secret to my grave. Five minutes after she was dead I'd have given every drop of blood to bring her back to life. I felt so sorry."

A cunning, cold blooded deed; a perfect concealment of the crime; after years, a revealing letter to the mother of the victim in a self-betraying envelope; now a mixture of unconcern and regret. What manner of man was this? And what was the social medium that fostered him?

Albert Howard Fish was born in Washington, D.C. in 1870. He came from a highly respected family. But an investigation of his pedigree showed that in his branch of the family there was considerable mental abnormality. In two generations seven people, apart from Fish himself, suffered from psychoses or were severely psychopathic personalities. One paternal uncle suffered from a "religious psychosis" and died in a state hospital. One was in Maine and the other was in California. A younger brother was feeble-minded and died of hydrocephalus. His mother was held to be "very queer"

9

and was said to have heard things on the street and to have seen things. (One juror told me after the trial: "That doesn't mean anything. I have an aunt who does that too.") A paternal aunt was considered "completely crazy." A brother suffered from chronic alcoholism. A sister had "some sort of mental affliction."

When Fish was five years old his father died and his mother, who was then working, had to place him in an orphanage. He was very unhappy there and "ran away every Saturday."

He was a fidgety, nervous child and suffered from enuresis until he was eleven. He graduated from public school at fifteen. At that time he took the name of Albert instead of his given name, Hamilton, because he was sensitive about being called "Ham" and "Ham-and-Eggs and all that" by the other boys at the school. He had been given the name Hamilton after a distant ancestor, Hamilton Fish, who was Secretary of State during President Grant's two terms of office and was often referred to as "the pillar of the administration." This ancestor had received the name from his father, who was an intimate friend and executor of Alexander Hamilton.

Fish's first jobs were in a grocery store. But soon he became apprenticed to a house painter and all through his life continued to do painting, decorating, and odd jobs of that kind.

At the age of twenty-eight he married a girl of nineteen. They had six children. When I saw him he had five grandchildren. After almost twenty years of marriage his wife left him, eloping with a man who boarded at their house. She "sold everything in the house" and left the children behind. (The youngest child was then three.) Fish cared for the children faithfully and conscientiously, as the children themselves agreed. "I acted as both father and mother to them," Fish put it.

Subsequently he entered into three marriages which were all illegitimate, inasmuch as he was never divorced.

At the time of his arrest for the Budd murder he had no steady work and he and the children lived in very poor circumstances. The detective who arrested him found the children in such need that he left them a dollar for food.

Fish's sexual life was of unparalled perversity. I did research in the psychiatric and criminal literature and found no published case that would even nearly compare with his. Freud has described the assumed primitive pleasure life of the infant as "polymorph perverse." In one of his latest (posthumous) papers he pointed out that when the different phases of the organization of the libido follow each other there are no sharp divisions, but instead a considerable overlapping. Fish was a polymorph perverse adult. There was no known perversion that he did not practice and practice frequently. I summarized them in a list designed for the court, eighteen perversion, or paraphilias, their technical names and their definitions. (This list was not admitted as evidence by the court; but it was seized upon avidly by the reporters present, who ere handicapped in their reporting by the fact that most of the material in evidence was literally not "fit to print.")

When Fish was five years old he had a woman teacher who used to spank the children frequently on their bare bodies. At that early age he used to derive sexual pleasure from having this done to him and from seeing it done to others.

Sado-masochism directed against children, particularly boys, took the lead in his sexual regressive development. "I always had a desire to inflict pain on others and to have others inflict pain on me. I always seemed to enjoy everything that hurt. The desire to inflict pain, that is all that is uppermost." Experiences with excreta of every imaginable kind were practiced by him, actively and passively. He took bits of cotton, saturated them with alcohol, inserted them in his rectum, and set fire to them. He also did that to his child victims. Finally, and clearly also on a sexual basis, he developed a craving going back to one of the archcrimes of humanity—cannibalism.

I elicited from him a long history of how he preyed on children. In many instances—I stated under oath later "at least a hundred"—he seduced them or bribed them with small sums of money or forced them and attacked them. His trade as a house painter served as a convenient prop. He often worked in public buildings and had an excuse for spending time in cellars and basements and even garrets. He would put on his painter's overalls over his nude body, and that permitted him to undress in a moment. It also prevented his victims—and any possible chance witnesses of his entrance or exits—from ever seeing him in his "regular clothes."

Most, if not all, of his victims came from poorer classes. He told me that he selected colored children especially, because the authorities didn't pay much attention when they were hurt or missing. For example, once he paid a small colored girl five dollars regularly to bring him little colored boys. His trade as a house painter gave him an excuse for changing his clothes in out-of-the-way places and working in many different localities. Frequently, after a particularly brutal episode he would change his address completely—move from one end of town to the other, or from one city to another, or from one state to another. He never returned to the same neighborhood. Altogether he roamed over twenty-three states, "from New York to Montana. And I have had children in every state." Often his employment was suddenly terminated "because things about these children came out."

Using address obtained from advertisements in magazines and from matrimonial agencies, he wrote innumerable obscene letters. They were not the typical obscene letters based on fantasies and daydreams to supply a vicarious thrill. They were offers to practice his inclinations with the people he wrote his graphic suggestions to. He would, for instance, write that he wanted to get in touch with a woman who would whip boys for and with him. One woman, who had received letters from him in answer to her advertisement for elderly people who needed convalescent care, told me that he had written to her and then come to see her. "He looked like an innocent man, but he had a rope or clothesline in a piece of wrapping paper and he said he wanted to be beaten with it. When he departed he left the rope." Her complaint to the advertising agency brought the response that they did not see anything to complain about!

In his letter and activities he used many aliases: for example, Frank Howard, John W. Pell, Robert Hayden, Thomas A. Sprague.

By painstaking and persistent examination, by checking data and by speaking with others who had personal contacts with him and with the facts, I made every effort to scrutinize his statements as to their veracity. There was one thing told me which I would not have believed, even though some of his children confirmed it, if I had not had absolutely irrefutable objective evidence of it.

Fish told me that for years he had been sticking needles into his body in the

Grace Budd

POLICE DEPARTMENT
CITY OF NEW YORK

Police Authorities are Requested to Post this Circular for the Information of Police
Officers and File a Copy of It for Future Reference

ARREST FOR KIDNAPPING

GRACE BUDD

FRANK HOWARD, Age, 58 years; height, 5 feet 7 inches; weight, 135 pounds; blue eyes; light complexion; mixed gray hair; small gray mustache which may be removed; teeth in poor condition three protruding upper teeth; slightly bow-legged; white; wore blue suit, black shoes, and soft black felt hat; large diamond ring; is a smooth talker and when last seen had considerable money on him.

This man called at the residence of Mr. and Mrs. Budd, 406 West 15th Street, New York City, on May 28, 1928, to make inquiries about Edward Budd, their 18 year old boy, who had advertised in the New York World for a position as a farm hand. Howard left the home of the Budds and came back the following Sunday, June 3, and while there saw Grace Budd, 10 year old daughter, and took her to attend a birthday party on West 137th Street, and neither of them has been seen since.

DESCRIPTION OF KIDNAPPED GIRL:

GRACE BUDD, Age, 10 years; height, 4 feet; weight, 60 pounds; large blue eyes; dark brown hair, bobbed straight; sallow complexion; anaemic; born in United States; white; residence, 406 West 15th Street, New York City. Wore light gray coat, gray fur on collar, cuffs, and down the front; white silk dress and socks; white pomps; gray silk hat with blue ribbon streamer from back; white pearl beads about neck; pink rose on lapel of coat; carried a brown pocketbook.

The photograph appearing on this circular does not answer the description of this girl, as to her clothing.

If arrested, immediately notify Detective Division, Police Headquarters, New York City, by telephone or telegraph, and an officer will be sent with necessary papers to cause his return to this jurisdiction.

Telephone Spring 3100

JOSEPH A. WARREN,
Police Commissioner.

region near his genitals, in the area between the rectum and the scrotum. He told of doing it to other people, too, especially to children. At first, he said, he had only stuck these needles in and then pulle dthem out again. They were needles of assorted sizes, some of them big sail needles. Then he had stuck others in so far that he was unable to get them out, and they stayed there. "They're in there now," he said. I asked him how many, and he said he didn't know. "I put them up under the spine. I took out only one needle. I couldn't get the others. I did put one in the scrotum, too; but I couldn't stand the pain."

I checked this strange story on a series of X-rays of his pelvic and abdominal region. They showed plainly twenty-nine needles inside his body. One X-ray of the pelvic region showed twenty-seven. They were easily recognizable as needles; in some instances the eyes of the needles were clear. Some of them must have been years in his body, for they were eroded to an extent that would have taken at least even years. Some of the needles were fragmented by this erosion so that only bits of the steel remained in the tissue. Their location showed that they had been inserted through the skin and not swallowed. Some were so deeply imbedded that they were in rather dangerous places: some just above and beside the transverse and descending colon, several fragments around the rectum, some in the region of the bladder. These X-rays are unique in the history of medical science.

One of his sons, questioned on this point, told me that he had found some of these needles cached in one of his father's books, a volume of stories by Edgar Allen Poe, in the story "The Narrative of A. Gordon Pym."

When Fish was in his middle fifties a definite psychosis with delusions and hallucinations began to develop insidiously. Always intensely interested in religion, he began to be engrossed in religious speculations about purging himself of iniquities and sins, atonement by physical suffering and self-torture, human sacrifices. At times he identified himself with God and felt that he should sacrifice his own son. He tried to stick needles under his fingernails but could not stand the pain. He made the poignant remark: "If only pain were not so painful!"

He had visions of Christ and His angels and saw Christ mumbling words which he couldn't understand. Sometimes he was sure the voices he heard came from visions and angels. Sometimes he didn't know where the voices came from. He heard them saying things like "stripes," "rewardeth," and "delighteth." And he connected these words with voices from the Bible and elaborated them delusionally with his sadistic wishes. "'Stripes' means to lash them, you know. I could hear words spoken, and of course a great deal I have read. I could put the words together and see what they meant. Then I made upt he rest from what I read." He would go on endlessly with quotations from the Bible all mixed up with his own sentences couched in biblical phraseology: "O ye daughter of Babylon"; "Blessed is he that rewardeth them as Thou servest us"; "Happy is he that taketh thy little ones and dasheth their heads against the stones"; "Blessed is the man who correcteth his son in whom he delighteth with stripes, for great shall be his reward."

He felt driven to torment and kill children. Sometimes he would gag them, tie them up, and beat them, although he preferred not to gag them, circumstances permitting, for he liked to hear their cries. He felt that he was ordered by God to castrate little boys. "I had sort of an idea through Abraham offering his son Isaac as a sacrifice. It always seemed to me that I had to offer a child for sacrifice, to purge myself of iniquities, sins, and abominations in the sight of God. Such a Sodom and Gomorrah!'"

He frequently "saw" a "human body being tortured—someone in hell." His hallucinations of hearing may have been accentuated by the fact that he developed real trouble with his hearing. He had episodes lasting a few minutes or sometimes more than a day during which he craved or executed his sadistic and autosadistic activities in a mental state of horror and rapture, of ecstasy and confusion, with or without hallucinations. Frequently he enjoyed these experiences (e.g., sticking needles into himself) to the point of orgasm.

Questioned about these needles, he gave me five conflicting—but to his mind apparently not contradictory—explanations. He said that he did it to relieve the pain from a hernia; that he "got a sexual kick out of it"; that he did it to punish himself for what he did to others; that "voices told me to purge myself of sin by self-torture, that's what induced me to put them in"; that by perforating his intestines they might kill him. His ideas of self-punishment took on more and more a religious character of expiation and atonement.

In the same way, in talking about the murder of grace Budd and his previous sadistic acts, he made no attempt to blame them on his supernatural messages. He said to me, "I am not insane. I am just queer. I don't understand it myself. It is up to you to find out what is wrong with me." He always mixed up his explanations when he talked about these messages, saying both that he had the desire to do something and that he was commanded to do something. These discrepancies in explanation never bothered him at all.

In this murder his designs were originally on the Budd boy, Grace's brother. He intended to castrate him. "They asked me if I didn't think it would be a fatal affair. I said, 'That would be a fatal affair.' I would have left him in the house, tied up, and gone back to my room, packed up my things and left town." This was no empty fantasy; this is precisely what he had done in previous cases where he had castrated or partly castrated small boys before this.

But the son was too big and didn't attract him, so when he saw Grace he thought only of her. "I knew this child would eventually be outraged and tortured and so forth." Is how he explained it, "and that I should sacrifice her in order to prevent her future outrage. The only interpretation of it that I could have was that she could be saved in that way."

On the train, he had with him a bundle containing a knife, a saw, and a cleaver—the "implements of hell," as he described them to me. When he got off the train he forgot to take them with him. "As soon as the train stopped at the station I had stepped off and was holding up my hands for her to jump in my arms. No thought of the tools. But she remembered that I had brought a package, sees my hands empty, says, 'Oh! You have forgotten your package!' and runs back to the seat where it had been left and gets it. Had she jumped in my arms when I said 'Jump!' instead of looking for the package, the waiting conductor would have given the signal to the engineer and the train would have gone on, carrying the tools out of my reach. The child would now be in her home and I would not be where I am."

15

This incident is similar to that which led directly to his capture by the police. For the letter he wrote to Mrs. Budd he used an envelope with a return address and the insignia of a protective association printed on it. He inked out the address only imperfectly, the insignia not at all. Though he took with him the "implements of hell" to kill and dismember Grace, he left them on the train when he got off; though he inked out the return address on the envelope he wrote to the mother of his child victim, he did so only partially. His Unconscious stepped in, in each instance, making him take steps tantamount to not killing Grace in that one instance, and to giving himself up in the other.

He gave a straightforward story of the crime. "I was in the house and took off my clothes an the other room. She picked flowers. I went to the window and called, 'Grace!' When she came in and saw me naked she screamed and said, 'I'll call Mama!' I grabbed her by the throat and almost carried her in the room and laid her on the floor. I didn't think she would put up such a struggle. She was a frail-looking child. She gave me the surprise of my life. She was losing consciousness, and I placed my knee on her chest to squeeze the breath out of her, to get her out of her misery." Then he dismembered her body, cutting off her head. In a posthumous paper discussing the severed head of the Medusa, Freud equates symbolically cutting off the head and castration. Fish, who had never read Freud, said in on of his six signed confessions to the police: "I thought it [Grace Budd] was a boy" (at the time of the murder).

He took parts of her body home with him, cooked them in various ways with carrots and onions and strips of bacon, and ate them over a period of nine days. During all this time he was in a state of sexual excitement. He ate the flesh during the day and thought about it during the nights.

His state of mind while he described these things in minute detail was a peculiar mixture. He spoke in a matter-of-fact way, like a housewife describing her favorite methods of cooking. You had to remind yourself that this was a little girl that he was talking about. But at times his tone of voice and facial expression indicated a kind of satisfaction and ecstatic thrill. I said to myself: However you define the medical and legal borders of sanity, this certainly is beyond that border.

Six years elapsed, during which he wore the same suit, continued his habitual behavior, and remained in the same vicinity. He did not even shave off the gray mustache which he had always worn and which was carefully described in the police circulars about him. When he was arrested it was as if he was expecting it. He greeted the detective like Stanley greeting Dr. Livingstone.

That was the private life of Albert Fish. But there was a public side to his life too. And that seemed to me the most important point of the story. It certainly would have been the most important to Grace Budd.

Fish was no stranger to the authorities. According to the official record, he had been arrested at least eight times. A federal probation report in 1930 listed six arrests, stating that for three of them the disposition was "not known." He was once in jail for grand larceny, having embezzled money while working in a store. That time he was paroled after sixteen months. He was arrested again, sent to the workhouse, and from there returned to state prison for violation of parole. For two arrests for false checks he received suspended sentences. For sending obscene letters through the mails he

16

was sentenced to ninety days and served twenty-five of them. Arrested for violation of probation, after having gone to a different state, he was again continued on probation for a short time. On no less than two occasions he was sent to psychiatric hospitals for observation.

In 1930 he was sent to a psychiatric hospital for observation for the first time. He stayed there for a whole month. This was two and a half years after he had killed and eaten Grace Budd. The Federal Court informed the hospital at that time that Fish's daughter had reported that he "at times showed signs of a mental disturbance." And while he was in the hospital a nurse made a special note of the fact that she saw him praying in the bathtub. Yet he was discharged to the court with the diagnosis of "not insane; psychopathic personality; sexual type." The Federal Court sentenced him to six months' probation.

The very next year the proprietor of a boarding school complained about obscene letters. This was in the summer of 1931. The police investigated and arrested Fish, who was working then as a handy man in a hotel. They searched his room and found there a cat-o'-nine-tails made of a stick and leather, of the type that he liked to use on himself and on children. He told police that he used it to whip himself. The detective noticed a "very, very weird look" on the defendants face and called and ambulance from a psychiatric hospital. The doctor who came examined Fish, pronounced him a mental case, and diagnosed him "sadism." So Fish was sent to a psychiatric hospital for a second time. This time he stayed for two weeks. The nurses reported times that he was "very restless" and "confused." But during his stay in the hospital no one asked him a word about the cat-o'-nine-tails, no investigation was made, and the one psychiatric examination that was carried out consisted of a thirteen-line superficial quotation of Fish's remarks and three words: "quiet, co-operative, oriented."

In addition to these arrests, confinement in jails and psychiatric hospitals, he was "picked up" innumerable times, usually for impairment of the morals of minors. Yet the attention of the authorities to this man, whom his family, many neighbors, and many past employers knew to be constantly after children, was neither penetrating nor persistent. Nobody ever made any attempt to pick up the pieces or put them together. At no time was he ever referred by anybody even to a mental hygiene clinic for examination or proper disposition. This was true although he made no secrets of his interests or of his predilections. When he was arrested for the Budd girl's murder he had in his grip a number of clippings about the Haarmann case, with photographs. Haarmann was a mass murderer in Hanover, Germany, who killed many young boys and sold their flesh as meat.

I asked him about these occasions when he was "picked up": how, when, what for, where? Although it was usually on account of a specific complaint about a child, "it never came out. Children don't seem to tell. I always managed to cover it up." In response to a question he said: "Once I was picked up for murder." He did not like to talk about that. He told me about attempts he made to castrate boys and how several times he had tried to do this to himself too. The year after the Budd murder "I had a boy of thirteen. On a Sunday afternoon I was leading him away from the home with the purpose to kill him and cut him up. I would have hit him on the head and then got the implements and cut what I wanted and then leave the rest out there. A number of

17

automobiles came along while I was still looking for the proper place. If it hadn't been for the passing automobiles, I would have killed him."

Then there was a little girl of twelve whom he met while he was doing a painting job in a home. "She was very loose in her ways, although only a child. I had her in my room, but what stopped me was the man who had a master key, showing the empty flats. I put her in a closet and put a fifty-pond paint pail in front of the closet. Otherwise I would have been in a fix right there. The manager said he had heard things. He felt like kicking me out. He must have heard the things from some of these children."

There was incident after incident over a period of decades. I came to the conclusion that he was responsible for a number of unsolved child murders and disappearances in New York and elsewhere. I had occasion to confirm this later, through the police. The detective who arrested Fish for the Budd murder stated later that Fish had committed three other child murders in New York City alone. At the time when he was picked up for one of these child murders he was released because he "looked so innocent"! On another occasion in another child murder case the motorman of a trolley car remembered and identified him as the man who was with a little boy who was crying all the time. This little boy was never seen again.

Following the opening address of the district attorney, the trial of Albert Fish proceeded in the customary manner, the prosecution and the defense presenting evidence and raising objections in the usual way. So much detail was in evidence that there was no reasonable doubt that Fish had killed the Budd girl and cut up her body. He had signed six confessions to that effect. The prosecution brought out all the details pointing to premeditation, deliberation, and intent. The defense demanded minute proof of each point and stressed his abnormality. The X-rays showing the needles in Fish's body were displayed, and every needle was counted and analyzed. Fish's children testified that they had seen him hitting himself on his nude body with a nail studded "paddle" until he was covered with blood. And they told how they had seen him stand alone on a hill with his hands raised shouting: "I am Christ!"

The corpus delicti was presented in the courtroom in a cardboard carton, and the district attorney frequently and dramatically rattled the bones both figuratively and actually. There was a great deal of quibbling about what the lawyers call immaterial and irrelevant matters.

The district attorney and the defense counsel referred in the course of their arguments to their respective war records in the Army and Navy until the court impatiently suggested that the court would concede that both had won World War I and that the trial should proceed from there.

There was a controversy about the relationship of full moons and madness, and the effect that a possibly full moon might have on Fish's mind, and the court was asked to take judicial cognizance of the phases of the moon, for which purpose a World Almanac was produced in court.

An anthropologist from John Hopkins University, called in to identify definitely the bones of the victim, had found an acorn carefully preserved along with the bones. That acorn appeared in the cross-examination of one of the medical witnesses: "Don't you know that among what were claimed to be human bones was an acorn? Isn't it a fact that an acorn was taken out of the box?"

There was discussion as to whether the photographs of the lonely scene of the murder taken by the police at night by the aid of flashlights were not too "gruesome" and shouldn't better have been taken by daylight.

The jurors seemed to listen with infinite patience but apparently made their own inner comments and reservations. One of them told me afterward that they had tabbed the lawyers with destructive nicknames. The district attorney was "Bones" (because he was constantly rattling them) and the defense counsel was "I-Object" (because of his frequent objections to points the district attorney attempted to introduce into evidence).

When I was called to the witness stand as psychiatric expert on behalf of the defense I outlined Fish's life, his abnormal mental make-up, and his mental disease, which I diagnosed as a paranoid psychosis. During much of my testimony the court asked the women to leave the courtroom on account of the nature of the material. I had to discuss and the discussions with Fish I had to cite.

I characterized his personality as introverted and extremely infantilistic. I pointed out that a child might be cruel to an insect, and might not know the difference between men and women, and might wish to play with his urine and feces without knowing what that means. But I have yet to see a man who did all these things and continued to do them up to the age of sixty-five as this man did. I gave it as my opinion that he had in one way or another attacked at least one hundred children, and said that I was convinced that the murder with which he was charged was not the only one he had committed.

The Rorschach test which I gave him in jail also indicated the presence of a psychosis and showed a most unusual and extreme preoccupation with infantilistic and perverse sexual images, coupled with some religious complexes.

In response to a hypothetical question that was fifteen thousand words long, covered forty-five typewritten pages, and took and hour and a half to be read, I declared that in my opinion Fish was legally insane. "He does not know the nature and quality of his acts. He does not know right from wrong. He is insane now and was insane then. His intellectual resources are not affected; that is true of the vast majority of insane people. Fish told me: 'What I did must have been right or an angel would have stopped me, just as the angel stopped Abraham in the Bible. If it was wrong, the angel would have stopped me.' A man who labors under delusions is not a free agent. He is not deterred by punishment."

I was cross-examined for hours. In response to the question about whether what Fish had told me were not just fantasies, I said that this was the first fantasy I had ever heard of that showed on an X-ray.

I was asked questions covering various angles of the law with respect to mental disease.

What is paranoid psychosis? It is a mental disease characterized primarily by delusional misinterpretations and in some cases by hallucinatory experiences with relative intactness of the reasoning powers of the intelligence.

Asked to classify mental diseases legally, I had to state that there is no legal classification of mental diseases, that diseases are classified only medically.

What is a psychopathic personality? A psychopathic personality is a vague term which means a mild kind of abnormality not gross enough to be called a mental disease, but which, on the other hand, does not permit one to call a man who has it completely normal. Many patients who are not mentally diseased, not insane, are therefore classified in a vague general way as psychopathic personality—which means only that they have an abnormal mental make-up. I gave it as my opinion that, quite apart from the later developing paranoid psychosis, Fish's mental makeup was so abnormal that on that alone, according to the mental hygiene law, one could and should have committed him long since to a civil state hospital. None of the facts that I stated, including the cannibalism, were contested. But my opinion about his legal insanity was challenged.

"Now doctor, insanity is a disease of the mind, isn't it?"

"No. Insanity is a legal term, a purely legal term, which in medicine has no meaning. There is no disease called insanity. Strictly speaking, a doctor cannot pronounce anybody insane. Only a court or jury can do that. A doctor can only say that a man suffers from a mental disease and that therefore he should be declared insane."

Having stated that in my opinion Fish did not know the difference between right and wrong in the sense of the statute, I was quizzed on that point. I stated that the knowledge of right and wrong is quite different from the knowledge that two plus two equals four. It requires intactness of the whole personality. Because Fish suffered from delusions and particularly was so mixed up about the questions of punishment, sin, atonement, religion, torture, self-punishment, he had a perverted, a distorted—if you want, an insane—knowledge of right and wrong. His test was that if it had been wrong he would have been stopped, as Abraham was stopped, by an angel.

When my definition of right and wrong was criticized as a "psychiatrist's" and not legal one, if the legal one is to have any real practical meaning—but there the district attorney interrupted me.

Two psychiatrists of high academic standing testified, from their own independent examinations, to the legal insanity of Fish on account of his paranoid psychosis. The State countered with four psychiatrists in rebuttal. Here was one of those legal battles of experts so often said to give a black eye to psychiatry. But that would not be so if the eyes of official psychiatry —and especially forensic psychiatry—were not already bloodshot.

All four psychiatric experts who testified in rebuttal proclaimed Fish sane. One of them was professionally associated with a district attorney's office. Another was a regular psychiatric adviser to the district attorney of the county. One was the chief of both of the public psychiatric hospitals where Fish had been "observed" some two years after the Budd (and other) murders—while he was still being sought "high and low" on that account by the police!—and there declared both harmless and sane.

All four agreed on the diagnosis of psychopathic personality, which one of them amplified by adding that "I should say that the proportion of those who walk the streets who are psychopathic personalities is at least 25 per cent, if not more." Two of these psychiatrists based their testimony on one joint interview they had with Fish one evening. One of them became so agitated and excited on cross-examination that the court had to declare a recess until he could collect himself enough to allow the trial to proceed.

Psychiatry is by no means so vague a science as some who do not know it, or who practice it unscientifically, like to assume. There are many well-established data.

For example, a patient will not talk about his delusions right off, or about his hallucinations either. Frequently they have to be elicited by careful, prolonged examination. Paranoid psychoses frequently remain unrecognized and undetected for a long time until a complete and competent psychiatric examination is carried out, based on subjective and objective data. Coprophagia is always an indication of mental disease, and cannibalism in our time, with the exception of extreme catastrophic hunger situations with impending death, is unthinkable for any person in his right mind. In psychiatric hospitals and in mental hygiene clinics it is customary to commit to state hospitals those individuals whose mental state is such that they are a danger to themselves or others.

These four psychiatrists who declared Fish sane made extraordinary statements under oath. For instance, they said the following:

"The family background of a patient is not always necessary. If I am insane, then my family history might help me—but if I am not sick, it is not necessary."

"There are cases that are obvious. If you look at them, you know they are insane."

"Danger has nothing to do with the commitment of mental cases [sic!]."

"Committing a crime has nothing to do with mental disease."

"Coprophagia is a common sort of thing [sic!]. We don't call people who do that mentally sick [sic!]. A man who does that is socially perfect all right [!]. As far as his social status is concerned, he is supposed to be normal, because the State of New York Mental Hygiene Department also approves of that [!]."

"They [people with coprophagia] are very successful people, successful artists, successful teacher, successful financiers."

"The bathtub in the hospital might have been a very good place for him to pray, if he wanted to pray."

"Paranoid individuals are usually rather frank and free and let things out rather easily [sic]."

"Well, a man might for nine days eat that [human] flesh and still not have psychosis. There is no accounting for taste."

"It is a matter of appetite and intensive satisfaction, and the individual may do very repulsive things and still be a seer, I mean a very wise man."

"I know of individuals prominent in society—one individual in particular that we all know. He ate human feces as a side dish with salad….I had a patient who was a very prominent public official who did it."

"I have not seen any cases laboring for years under a psychosis without it being ascertained."

"In his psychosis there would not be any lucid intervals. He either has it or he hasn't it."

"I did not ask him anything about that sort of thing—inflicting pain on himself in order to obtain sexual pleasure."

"One finds within about half an hour that the patient has paranoia."

"If a man takes alcohol and puts it on cotton and puts that into his person and sets fire to it, that is not masochistic; he is only punishing himself and getting sex grat-

21

Grace Budd with her brother and sister.

Height 4 Feet
— Last seen wearing white felt hat blue streamer in back.
— Hair dark, straight bobbed.
Eyes blue
Complexion sallow.
Physical condition anaemic.
Last seen wearing pink rose here.
Last seen wearing gray overcoat. with fur collar and cuffs. and down front of coat.
Last seen carrying brown pocket book.
Last seen wearing white silk dress.

Last seen wearing white silk socks.

Last seen wearing white shoes.
Age 10 Years
Weight 60 Lbs.

Grace Budd

23

ification that way."

"When a man is sexually abnormal, he is sexually abnormal and is liable to go to all extremes."

In describing Fish's sticking needles into himself and into children, I had used the technical term, "picqueur acts." Questioned about this one, one of these experts stated airily that "oh yes," he knew all about that; a picqueur is one who peeks and "peeking didn't mean a thing"!

The most eloquent psychiatric testimony—unknown to the jury—was given without a word being spoken. The psychiatrist who had been in charge of Fish's case on the ward during one of his stays in a psychiatric hospital left the city, with the knowledge of the authorities, during the period of the trial.

When the trial was coming to a close the reporters at the press table held a poll among themselves and came to the conclusion that Fish was legally insane. The jury thought otherwise, pronounced him guilty, and he was sentenced to the electric chair—a sentence which the Court of Appeals upheld. Later one of the jurors commented that most of them felt that Fish was insane but should be electrocuted anyhow.

When his lawyer visited Fish for the last time in the death house in Sing Sing, just before making an appeal to the governor for commutation of the death sentence, Fish "talked to me about all his sexual and religious ideas and gave me documents so obscene that I couldn't show them to anybody."

A short while before the date was set for the execution I received an invitation from the counsel to the governor to appear at a governor's hearing concerning Albert Fish. It was a cold afternoon in January when I went to the stately room where the hearing was held. The district attorney and members of his staff were there, the counsel for the defense and his associates and five of Fish's children—two daughters and three sons. There were a few other people present, most of whom I did not know. Facing this small audience was a large desk with two chairs behind it. Presently the governor and his counsel entered and sat down there.

The counsel for the defense pleaded for commutation of the death sentence and confinement in a state institution for the criminal insane. He told the governor that when the case was argued before the Court of Appeals the chief judge had remarked that "there is no doubt that this man is insane; but the question is, does he come within the legal definition of insanity?" "You, Your Excellency, are not bound by the legal definitions of insanity."

The district attorney asked for the death penalty. "This is one case in which I cannot see one single fact that deserves leniency on your part."

When it was my turn to address the governor I stood before the desk and gave a brief outline of the case. I said that no more concrete objective evidence of a man's mental abnormality could possibly be demonstrated than the X-rays in this case. I said I was not appealing on behalf of Mr. Fish, who didn't mind the electric chair anyway, in his distorted ideas of atonement. He was, in my opinion, a man not only incurable and unreformable, but also unpunishable. I was appealing on behalf of his many child victims, I was also appealing on account of the many victims, past and future, of such men as Fish.

Most of the victims, I went on—if not all of them—belonged to the poorer classes of the population. Many of them were Negroes. All of them were unprotected by the present setup. Years ago this man could have—and should have—been confined permanently in a state hospital for mental diseases. I pointed out that in the two months preceding the trial I myself had made out commitment papers for more than one hundred and sixty patients without any court hearing. And many of them had not been so sick as Albert Fish, and none of them so dangerous.

"If you uphold the judgment of sanity implicit in the death sentence of this obviously ill man," I continued, "you uphold, officially, the policy of psychiatrists who on two different occasions have had under observations a man who had butchered and eaten more than one little child more than two years before, and who have the temerity to declare now that such a man was not a suitable case for commitment to an institution for the insane. Assume what might easily have been possible: through some technicality, say a doubt about the identity of the corpus delicti (of which only bones remained) had existed, and this case had to be dropped legally. Are you as a statesman telling me as a psychiatrist that I have no right to commit this man to an institution for the insane? And that the community has to wait until he has tortured and killed still another child—and been caught—before it can safeguard itself? The choice before you is whether you want to endorse abstruse psychiatric sophistries or the efforts of those who want to see that the children of the community will be protected in the future.

"To execute a sick man is like burning witched," I went on. "The time will come when psychiatrists will be as little proud in their role in these procedures as the theologians are of their role in the past.

"Science is prediction. The science of psychiatry is advanced enough that with proper examination such a man as Fish can be detected and confined before the perpetration of these outrages, instead of inflicting extreme penalties after ward. The authorities had this man, but the records show that they paid no attention.

"A man who practices cannibalism under these circumstances has a deranged mind. I have spent much more time examining this man than all the prosecution psychiatrists combined. If he is electrocuted as sane, then you—to whose personal conscience the law entrusts this case at this moment—will give your stamp of approval to all the callousness and unconcern of those whose duty it was to protect the children of the community.

"It is not as an expert that I am appealing to you," I said, "because if you had all the facts assembled, including the other murders committed by this defendant, and their circumstances, you would not need an expert. I am not appealing to you for clemency. I am appealing to you as a statesman. In this case all the hairsplitting about legal definitions was just a covering up of a social default. I am asking you to commute the death sentence to lifelong detention in an institution for the criminal insane—and to make this case an example and a starting point for a real scrutiny not of individuals nor individual institutions, but of the whole haphazard and bureaucratic chaos of the psychiatric prevention of violent crimes."

All the time I was speaking, the counsel, who was sitting at the governor's left hand, followed me with the closest attention. He frequently nodded, as if in approval; he smiled at times; at times he showed that he was seriously moved. His whole manner encouraged me to go on.

But the governor just sat. His face betrayed nothing, no shade of feeling, no interest. I looked at him again and again, trying to figure out whether to continue or to stop. He was completely impassive.

I had never spoken to a governor before. All my professional life I had had experiences with lower officials who had either no interest or no power to land an ear to human suffering. That time in the state building at the capital I had had an image of an occasion where the very law specified that a high authority had to sit in his capacity as a human being, using his personal judgment to listen and decide. That was an old tradition that used to be jealously guarded by emperors and kings. These rulers on such occasions rose above the feudal lords and their vassals. I felt that this was the opportunity for once to reach the ear of a human being in authority. But I didn't succeed. When I had finished the governor rose, half nodded, and left the room, followed by his counsel. His impassive face remained with me—the symbol of cries unheard.

On the day f the execution of Albert Fish, Warden Lawes, one of America's most distinguished criminologists, hung on the telephone all evening in the hope of hearing from the governor. Asked what his feeling was about the execution of such a man, he replied: "I am not supposed to feel. I am just part of the apparatus."

One of the witnesses described the execution to me. Fish was calm and completely self-possessed. He walked into the execution chamber, coolly surveyed all the assembled witnesses, and assisted the attendants in strapping the electrical apparatus to his leg.

About two years later a member of Fish's family came to see me. He was unemployed and asked me to help him to get a job. We talked about Albert Fish. I explained to him that what he had was an illness like any other. The illness itself was no disgrace; the disgrace lay in its handling. And then I asked him how many children he thought Fish killed.

In my opinion there were at least five; one of the detectives had told me he had murdered at least eight; a judge of the Supreme Court who had been present when I testified had told me he had been reliably informed that Fish was implicated in fifteen child murders.

"You have been with him for so many years," I said. "Now that it's all over, what do you really think?"

He looked me straight in the eyes and answered: You know, Doctor, there were plenty of old, abandoned places. He'd always prowl around. It's hard to tell how many he killed."

And that is the way the authorities left it, too. They did not even count the victims.

Albert Fish is dead. The Fish case is settled. But it has always remained in my mind as unfinished business. A number of times since then I have had occasion to talk about such cases and problems to high officials who had the power to decide and act. I have looked for faces and found only masks. And masks have no ears.

PART II

Bellevue Reports and Non Mailable Matters

January 8, 1931

In re Albert H. Fish

Hon. Frank J. Coleman
U.S. District Court, So. Dist. of N.Y.

My dear Judge Coleman:

The following are the findings in the case of the above named defendant, Albert H. Fish, who was committed to the Psychopathic Department of Bellevue Hospital on December 15, 1930 for examination and observation.

As a result of psychiatric examination, we are of the opinion that this man at the present time is not insane, nor is he a mental defective.

While under observation in this hospital he has been quiet and co-operative; has conducted himself in an orderly and normal manner; there is no evidence of delusional notions nor hallucinatory experience. It is true that he shows some evidence of early senile changes; this condition, however, is quite slight at the present time and has not impaired his mentality. His memory, particularly for a man of his years, is excellent.

Although not insane, he exhibits a condition of Sexual Psychopathy, (sex perversion), as evidenced by his writing obscene letters to various individuals. Such conduct frequently is the result of senile dementia and is observed in men of advanced years, but in this particular case we believe it has not the same significance, for the reason that this man, according to the history, as well as our examination, has manifested sex perversion from early life, and further that, as already stated, psychiatric examination does not reveal any mental deterigration or dementia.

General physical examination does not reveal any serious changes, beyond some Arterio Selerosis and mild Nephritic disorder, which are not of serious nature at the present time.

To sum up:- This man, although abnormal (Psychopatic Personality) has, at the present time, sufficient mental capacity to know the nature and the quality of his acts and to differentiate between right and wrong.

Very truly yours,
M.S. GREGORY, DIRECTOR

29

CITY OF NEW YORK

DEPARTMENT OF HOSPITALS

BELLEVUE HOSPITAL

SOCIAL SERVICE DEPARTMENT

193
1117

Albert Fish

Depositing none-mailable matter in the U.S. Mails.

Coleman

Previous Record:

1903 - Sentenced 2 to 11 years in Sing Sing for Grand Larceny -
2nd degree. Paroled April 20, 1905. Returned to Randalls
Island March 8, 1906, and released on October 10, 1906.

7/31/28 - Attempted grand larceny in New York City - no disposition
known.

8/12/28 - New York City - Petit larceny - disposition unknown
8/22/28 - Attempted grand larceny New York City - disposition unknown.
5/2/30 - Held for investigation U.S. Detention Headquarters.
7/3/30 - Violation Sec. 211 U.S.C. Sentenced to 90 days. Sentence
commutted by Judge Patterson after 25 days.

Indictment - Violation of Sec. 211 U.S.C.C. Depositing none-mailable
matters in U.S. Mails.

Offense - On or about Sept. 19,1930, the defendant placed in the
Post Office for the purpose of delivery by the Post Office
of the United States a letter addressed to Mrs. E. Solared,
245 E. 40th St., New York City, containing matter of vile,
filthy and obscene nature.

State of complainant:

That this is a Psychopathic case and that the defendant
should be under observation.

Statement of Defendant:

Defendant states that he had carried on correspondence through
a matrimonial agency with several women scattered throughout
the country and that he had received obscene letters from
many of these women and thus fell into the habit of writing
filthy letters.

Aggravating and Mitigating Circumstances:

The fact that the defendant had served a term in the U.S.
Detention Headquarters for a similar offense during the past
aggravates the case.

The possibility that the defendant is unbalanced mentally
would mitigate the offense.

Personal History: Defendant is 60 years of age and was born in Washington, D.C. He comes from a respectable family. Defendant, his father and brother, have served enlistments in the U.S. Army and Navy yearss ago. Defendant's wife had been dead for about 15 years. Has 2 daughters and 2 sons living in Astoria, L.I. One daughter, Mrs. Anna Collins, states that the defendant has lived with her or her sister for a good many years and that they were not aware of his activities thru the matrimonial agency. She further states that her father was very good to them as children and provided for them to the best of his ability.

She states that her father had been helpful around the house in later years, but at times showed signs of a mental disturbance.

Both the defendant and his family are willing to have a mental observation made.

Physical and Mental Condition:

Defendant has suffered a great many years from a hernia but had this corrected at Bellevue Hospital in 1928. He is not strong physically. His mental condition is questionable.

Employment: Defendant is a painter by trade and spent considerable time in Government service. He has also served as sexton in various churches around New York.

Diagnosis: Defendant is a man well along in years, who made a practise of corresponding with women through a matrimonial agency. His family though not well to do are in comfortable circumstances, and are willing to care for him in the home of a married daughter.

Prognosis: Defendant's mental condition is doubtful and it is recommended that he be committed by the Court to Bellevue Hospital for observation.

Respectfully submitted.

Probation Officer

IMB

31

Name   Albert Fish   Admitted 12/15/30   4 P.M.

Bodily condition (Gen. nutrition, cleanliness, vermin, etc).

      Fairly well nourished. .Clean.

Physical Disorder (Deformities, Ruptures, Fractures, Dislocations, Contusions, Scars, Eruptions, etc.)

      Old scar on top of head.
      Vac. mark left arm.

Marks of Identification: Color of Hair and eyes.

      Peculiar Scars, tattoo marks, Peculiarities of Nose, ears and mouth deformities.

      Apparent Height and Weight.

Height: 5 ft. 7 in.

Weight   130 lbs.

Eyes   Brown

Hair   Gray

CITY OF NEW YORK

DEPARTMENT OF HOSPITALS

BELLEVUE HOSPITAL
SOCIAL SERVICE DEPARTMENT

December 17,1930

Re: Albert Fish
alias Robert Fiske, Sr.
C76-53
U.S. Dist. Court

Indicted for depositing non-mailable matters in U.S. Mails in
violation of Section 211 U.S.C.C. By attorney Robert Manley,
Jacob H. Morris, Acting as foreman.
Filed Dec. 8, 30

Dec. 9,30   Filed in open Court and defendant pleads guilty on Dec.
12.   Referred to U.S. Probation Officer H.R. Dean (Cert. 7-1355)

CASE

Southern District of New York SS.   The Grand Jurors for U.S. of A.
duly empanelled and sworn to in U.S. Court on the 19th of Sept.
at Southern Dist. of N.Y. and within the jurisdiction of this
Court, Albert H. Fish, alias Robert Fiske, Sr., the defendant herein,
did unlawfully, willfully, and knowingly cause to be taken from
U.S. Mails for the purpose of delivery by the Post Office Establishment
of U.S. to address indicated on the envelope in So. Dist. of N.Y.
and within jurisdiction certain unmailable matters, to wit: a letter
containing matter of such vile, filthy and obscene nature that to
set of the contents thereof herein, would defile the records of this
court, such vile, obscene letters having been written and mailed
by defendant addressed to divers persons at divers places to Grand
Jurors, unknown and that the said defendant did on or about the 19th
day of Sept. cause to be taken from the U.S. Mails and delivered by
Post Office Est. of U.S. in So. Dist. of N.Y. and within the
jurisdiction of this Court a certain such letter prepaid
with U.S. postage stamp for transmission and delivery by U.S. mails
and addressed in words and figures as follows:

Mrs. E. Selarid, 245, E. 40th St. N.Y.City. Apt. 14.   Said
letter containing writing or obscene lewd, lascivious, filthy and
indecent character against the peace of the U.S. and their dignity
and contrary to the form of the statute of U.S. in such case and
provided in Section 211 U.S.C.C.

Social Worker   M

B. Reilly

33

Abstracts of Letters

1. **Letter sent to Mr. Owen Keene.**

    Asks clemency on the grounds that (1) he is too old to obtain work and that enforced idleness has made him write the letters:
    (2) He has always taken care of his children.
    (3) His wife ran off and left him and now has 3 illegitimate children.

    (4) He does not drink, chew or smoke.

2. **Letter to Mrs. Ralston   Apr. 3, 1929**

    Relates that his mother and father used to spank each other severely on the bare buttocks and that he was 22 when he got his last spanking from his mother. H e would gladly take one again from her. He is in the motion picture business and many women wish to marry him but he wants the kind which is willing to whip a man. She must not hesitate to whip his boys when they are naughty. They are to be stripped naked and spanked on the buttocks. His boys have beautiful bodies and one has "something to whip". As a matter of justice, however, he must be spanked first. He will also spank her. This is in accordance with an "order" to which he belongs.

3. **Letter to Mrs. Ralston   Apr. 4, 1929.**

    He says in reply to her intimations that the spankings are done in a joke, that it is a perfectly serious matter. He proposes to bring the boys to board with her while her husband is away. He will slip into her bed. Her husband will not live forever. He (R.A.F.) will pay her $100 a week. He has a great deal of money and she will be well taken care of. He repeats that he wishes her to whip his boys, but in accordance with the rules of the order, he is to be stripped naked and spanked first. He will also whip her and kiss her buttocks.

4. **Letter to Mrs. Ralston   Date?**

    No one is ashamed to see a naked man. Many women wish to undress and spank him but this is reserved only for her. When she undresses one of his boys he will cover his "dickey" with his hands but not he. His "Dickey" belongs to her. She and her "tail" too, belong to him. He will strip her, spank her "behind" and suck "#2" out of it. She has a very sweet "ass" by the looks of her picture. His "Peter" and his "Peanuts" of which he has two and his ass belong to her. She has never been loved the way he will love her. When he sees her "big fat sweet behind" he will eat it up. They will do it in every way."

5. **Letter to Miss Watkins (colored) Apr. 30, 1930.**

    He is a widower, has a beautiful home in the country and is an artist who paints nude men and women. Boys are his favorites, ages 6-20. He has one model who is beautiful and has marvelous buttocks. His wife was a colored maid and his son was hers. The models are both colored and white. Boys and girls often climb up the fence to peep at the naked models. When they are bad he spanks their bare behinds. Saturday afternoon the models go and he strips naked and allows the maid to spank him. He also spanks her. Modesty does not pay the rent and there are plenty of girls willing to do these things.

34

6. Letter to ----   Sept. 19

        She has a very sweet face and he already loves
her. Two out of three living together are not married.
His parents were very strict. They were "free thinkers".
If the children did wrong, regardless of age or sex they
were stripped naked and received a severe whipping. At 18
he did "it" to a colored girl and his conscience has
bothered him so much since that he will not be satisfied
until he receives the whipping he would have got at that time
from his father. He must be spanked by a woman. His wife
died in 1917 and he has not been in bed with a woman since
then. She can give him the whipping he desires and then he
belongs to her. He cannot do anything until she strips
and whips him.

7. Letter (#2) to ----   Sept. 19.

        He was struck speechless when he saw her. She
must have noticed it. He has a brother-in-law who works in
Hollywood, who tells him that the women there make the men show
they love them. They make their husbands drink their "#1"
and eat their "#2" and leave them if they do not comply. He
will do this for her. His wife and he did the same thing.
Everybody does. What fun they will have in bed at night.
People live only once.

        A colored woman who knew his father wished to do
it to him (pt) but he never let her do it. Almost any
woman would strip a man naked and whip his behind until it
bled. He cannot do anything until she does so! He
sends her love, kisses and his "Dickey".

Early Mugshot of Albert Fish.

Development of Psychoses	Development of Intemperate Habits
Change in disposition, habit disorganizations, hallucinations, illusions or delusions, memory defect, excitement, suicidal or homicidal tendencies, etc.	Alcohol, morphine, cocaine, heroin etc. Age, moderate or excessive at first, periodic or continuous following illness or nervous breakdown, episodic outbreaks, delirium, hallucinosis, etc.

12-16-30

    C N T   evidentially neg.

12-16-30 - age nets

AD - 16/25 - can improve with lenses
OS   16/25 plus
No external eye pathology
muscle balance good
some early lens changes
Fundi: Early sclerosis of vessels
Suggest: Glasses for reading.

Send to Clinic after discharge.

- -

Physical Examination:

    Fairly well nourished, well developed, male of about 65.
    skin loose and wrinkled.

    Head: Scalp - negative
             Ears - Drums negative. No mastoid tenderness.
             Nose - No obstruction; septum intact.
             Mouth - No teeth, mucous membranes normal.

    Throat and Pharynx - negative.
    Lymph-glandular system - no general or local enlargement.
    Lungs - resonant and clear throughout
    Heart - not enlarged to percussion. No murmurs.
    Abd: Negative.
    Reflexes: Normal. Babinski - negative.
                Pupils slightly irregular, equal in size,
                react sluggishly to light, more promptly
                to accommodation.
    Peripheral blood vessels palpable, no marked sclerosis
    Blood pressure 156/80
    Fundi-vessels tortuous, beginning sclerosis.

- -

    Patient's Statement: "I've been arrested since November 20,
    1930 for sending obscene matter through the mail. I just sent
    one letter to a married woman in New York. We exchanged obscene
    letters. Her husband made a complaint to the post office
    authorities. I've known this woman since April. I've been
    arrested before in 1928 for Grand Larceny. I was placed on
    probation on the understanding that I would make restitution.
    I pleaded guilty to the charge."

Brought by officer from Court - with order.

Patient is quite agreeable, oriented - no apparent
delusions.

"I feel all right - I am weak - I have pain across
the back - I have never been sick in my life -
I never had a doctor."
                                        O.B

Officer states that charge involves sending obscene
matter and letters thru mails to women."
                                        O.B.

Att. states patient writes letters to people that he does not know, stating he is sect. of some wealthy man. He wants them to look after his children. He wants children to be wacked every day and whipped.

A. Nichols.

8-28-31

"I was picked up while working in a hotel in Rockaway on a paint job. Two detectives came there yesterday & said a man named Roach a complaint. I had written him a letter 2 wks. ago for a fellow named Erickson who couldn't write English. It was in reference to his children whom he was having trouble managing. I saw in the paper that Roach had a summer school for boys. So I wrote the letter asking if he would accept the boys there and that the father wanted them whipped. He had whipped them & had gotten into trouble with the Children's Society. The only other letters that I wrote to people I didn't know were thru a Matrimonial Ad. Bureau. I've been advertising since Apr. I've gotten answers but nothing satisfactory. I wanted one who had a little farm. I statedI was a man of good habits and had a trade. I have no enemies. I don't want to be dependent upon my sons-in-law".

Pt. quiet, cooperative, oriented.

Pupils react - K.K. pres. H.L.A. neg.

J.C.

Department of Hospitals:
Psychiatric Division
Bellevue Hospital

A B S T R A C T

Name: Albert H. Fish
                  129 Franklin Street, Astoria

Correspondent: Daughter-Mrs. Gertrude De Marco, same address.

Age: 61, white.

Birthplace: Washington, D. C.

Occupation: Painter

Schooling: Very little.

Admitted: December 15, 1930.

Discharged: January 6, 1931.

DIAGNOSIS: No Psychosis. Psychopathic Personality; Sexual
                  Psychopathy. Moderate Arteriosclerosis; Chr. Int.
                  Nephritis.

- - - - - -

Patient was committed to the Psychiatric Department of
Bellevue Hospital on December 15, 1930, by Judge Coleman, United States
District Court, charged with "Sending Obscene Matter Thru the Mail".

Patient's Statement: "I've been arrested since November
20, 1930 for sending obscene matter through the mail. I just sent one
letter to a married woman in New York. We exchanged obscene letters. Her
husband made a complaint to the post office authorities. I've known this
woman since April. I've been arrested before in 1928 for Grand Larceny.
I was placed on probation on the understanding that I would make
restitution. I pleaded guilty to the charge".

Physical Examination: Fairly well nourished, well
developed, male of about 66. Skin loose and wrinkled.
Head: Scalp - negative.
        Ears - Drums negative. No mastoid tenderness.
        Nose - No obstruction; septum intact.
        Mouth - No teeth, mucous membranes normal.
Throat and Pharynx - negative.
Lymph-glandular system - no general or local enlargement.
Lungs - resonant and clear throughout
Heart   not enlarged to percussion. No murmurs.
Abd: Negative.
Reflexes; Normal. Babinski - negative.
        Pupils slightly irregular, equal in size, react
        sluggishly to light,more promptly to accommodation.
Peripheral blood vessels palpable, no marked sclerosis.
Blood pressure 156/80/
Fundi-vessels tortuous, beginning sclerosis.

Spinal tap - clear fluid, 8 cells per cm, faint globulin.

Colloidal Gold 0011210000

Blood Chemistry - N P N 35, Sugar 85

Spinal Fluid / Wass. - negative

Blood Wassermann - negative.

Daughter's Statement: "He was arrested a few days before Thanksgiving. I don't know exactly why he was arrested. He acted alright to me. He has been living by himself in a furnished room since September. My mother died fourteen years ago. There were six children. He took quite an interest in us. Beginning about 2-3 years ago he began to live by himself. During the past year he has been unable to find steady employment. Before that he had always managed to find fairly regular employment as a painter. Lately we noticed that he didn't want to be bothered but he was always interested in the family. His memory was good. He wasn't unreasonable. He still continued to be considerate. A few days before he was arrested he seemed worried; said it would be a poor Thanksgiving for him".

RONTGEN RAY EXAMINATION

"No pathology of the skull
Sella turcica is normal.
Marked pathology of right maxillary".

PREVIOUS RECORD

1903 - Sentenced 2 to 11 yrs in Sing Sing for Grand Larceny-2nd Degree. Paroled April 20, 1905. Returned to Randall's Island, March 8, 1906 and released on October 10, 1906.

7/21/28 Attempted Grand Larceny - N.Y.C. - No disposition known.

8/12/28 New York City - Petit Larceny - Disposition unknown.

8/22/28 Attempted Grand Larceny - N. Y. C. - disposition unknown.

5/2/30 Held for Investigation - U.S. Detention Headquarters.

7/3/30 Violation Sec. 211 U.S.C.-sentenced to 90 days. Sentence commuted by Judge Patterson after 25 days.

RORSCHACH TEST   Feb.24, 1935

Albert Fish, 64 years old.   (FHW)

I.   1. Head of an owl; that's the eye. (Shadow. light + dark, (Small.

     2. Saw with broken, uneven teeth.

     3. The body of a man (center), arms, shoulders, neck, rectum. (W)

     4. Penis of a boy. (lower center).

II. 1. Two bears holding something on their snouts. (black).

     2. Faces, these red things -- some sort of goblin or devil --
            Faces I see sometimes at night, those red things.
     3. Claw of crab or lobster. (W)

     4. Someone doing #2. W

     5. That reminds me of a penis, I shd judge of a young man.
     6. Boy's testicles (W)
                                      or minstrels)
III. 1. Two men, dressed as waiters, putting something into a
            dish or pot.
         -- very long pause --
     2. Rectum. (upper light; center).

     3. Red bow necktie.
                                                    + male
     4. Small parrot (red at sides); no, like the face∧ of an ape;
(Delay ++) Some kind of devil (on other side).
                                    (head in center)
IV.∧ 1. Combination of elephant, wrong ears, though, and two
            large feet (at side) like gorilla feet.

     2. Face of some kind of an animal, ox, maybe. (Poorly seen, Rack + a
                                                       at lower center).
     3. Snake. (L)

     4. Man doing #2.
.'(Delay +++)
V.∧ 1. Butterfly's horns.

     2. Leg, like person's leg.

     3. Same, on other side.

     4. Pair of tongs (Bottom).

VI. Wh 1. Huge butterfly, wings spread.

     2. Skin of some animal; no head; front + hind paws.

     3. Udder of cow. (small edge; , back seen.

4. Bag hanging down, like a stocking filled with something. (*v. poorly seen*)

5. Some sort of a pole (whole center portion).

6. Two light things (center) remind me of something-- just can't say what it is.

7. Huge fish.

(*Delay ++++*)

VII. ^ 1. Pelvis of child. (*small upper center*) (*side*)

2. Whole thing: sponges growing under water, attached to each other, *like I seen at school*.

3. Face of an elephant. (*centre*)

Blue
VIII. 1. ^ Shoulders, white collar, no head.

2. ^ Someone doing #2. (*orange, lower*)

3. Some sort of small animal (pink); *chipmunk*.

(*Long, long pause + study*)
4. Someone sitting on ground, legs spread out (gray)

(*V. marked delay*)
IX. ^ 1. Large candle (center)..

(*2 gray things*)—
2. ^ Like a sewer coming together, skeleton of a child coming out. [*N. G. no forms*].

3. Pile of bones. (*Pink!*)

No:
4. ^ Top is head of a man; the rest just a pile of bones. (*!*)

5. Two parrots facing one another. (*yellow*) (*Seen from side.*)
sitting on the limb of a tree.

6. Face of a tiger, eyes looking at me. (*v. poorly seen.*)

7. Right and left hips -- a behind; the spine is just above here.

(*long delay*)*
X. ^ 1. Two blue octopuses, legs all around.

(*Red things:*) (*one half each side*)
2. ^ Body split in half; like loins of pork.

3. Different kinds of insects, *these other things.*

4. Part of a backbone. (*center gray*). (*This after hard study.*)

- *All prisoner's responses given after long contemplation, deliberation + turning of the picture. Always ends with, "Well that's all I can get out of that." All forms very poorly seen.*

PART III

FISH'S OWN WORDS

KIDNAPED AND KILLED BUDD GIRL, HE ADMITS

SAW MILL RIVER PARKWAY TO ELMSFORD

MOUNTAIN ROAD

MURDER HOUSE

WHERE FISH FORMERLY LIVED

My dear Mrs Budd

In 1894 a friend of mine shipped as a deck hand on the Steamer Tacoma, Capt John Davis. They sailed from San Francisco for Hong Kong China. On arriving there he and two others went ashore and got drunk. When they returned the boat was gone. At that time there was a famine in China. Meat of any kind was from $1 - to 3 Dollars a pound. So great was the suffering among the very poor that all children under 12 were sold to the Butchers to be cut up and used for food in order to keep others from starving. A boy or girl under 14 was not safe in the street. You could go in any shop and ask for steak - chops - or stew meat. Part of the naked body of a boy or girl would be brought out and just what you wanted cut from it. A boy or girls behind which is the sweetest part of the body and sold as veal cutlet brought the highest price. John staid there so long he acquired a taste for human flesh. On his return to N.Y. he stole two boys one 7 one 11. Took these to his home stripped them naked tied them in a sack then burned everything they had on. Several times every day and night he spanked them - tortured them - to make their meat good and tender. First he killed the 11 yr old boy, because he had the fattest ass and I assume the most meat on it. Every part of his body was

cooked and eaten except head - bones and guts. He was roasted in the oven, (all of his ass) boiled, broiled, fried, stewed. The little boy was next, went the same way. At that time I was living at 409 E 100 st. near - right side. He told me so often how good human flesh was I made up my mind to taste it. On Sunday June the 3 - 1928 I called on you at 406 W 15St. Brought you pot cheese - strawberries. We had lunch. Grace sat in my lap and kissed me. I made up my mind to eat her. On the pretense of taking her to a party. You said Yes she could go. I took her to an empty house in Westchester I had already picked out. When we got there, I told her to remain outside. She picked wild flowers. I went up stairs and stripped all my clothes off. I knew if I did not I would get her blood on them. When all was ready I went to the window and called her. Then I hid her in a closet until she saw the room. When she saw me all naked she began to cry and tried to run down stairs. I grabbed her and she said she would tell her mama. First I stripped her naked. How she did kick bite and scratch. I choked her to death, then cut her in small pieces so I could take my meat to my rooms, cook and eat it. How sweet and tender her little ass was roasted in the oven. It took me 9 days to eat her entire body. I did not fuck her tho I could of had I wished. She died a virgin

The following letter was written by Albert Fish and sent to the mother of Grace Budd on November 11, 1934. Mailing the letter would ultimately lead to Fish's arrest.

My Dear Mrs. Budd,

In 1894 a friend of mine shipped as a deck hand on the steamer Tacoma, Capt. John Davis. They sailed from San Francisco to Hong Kong China. On arriving there he and two others went ashore and got drunk. When they returned the boat was gone. At that time there was a great famine in China. Meat of any kind was from $1-3 dollars per pound. So great was the suffering among the very poor that all children under 12 were sold to the butchers to be cut up and sold for food in order to keep others from starving.

A boy or girl under 14 was not safe in the street. You could go in any shop and ask for steak- chops- or stew meat. Part of the naked body of a boy or girl would be brought out and just what you wanted cut from it. A boy or girls behind, which is the sweetest part of the body and sold as veal cutlet, brought the highest price- John staid there so long he acquired a taste for human flesh.

On his return to New York, he stole two boys one 7, one 11. Took them to his home stripped them naked tied them in a closet. Then burned everything they had on. Several times every day and night he spanked them- tortured them- to make their meat good and tender. First he killed the 11 year old boy because he had the fattest ass and of course the most meat on it. Every part of his body was cooked and eaten except, head- bones and guts. He was roasted in the oven, all of his ass, boiled, broiled, fried, stewed. The little boy was next went the same way. At that time I was living at 409 E. 100th Street, rear- right side. He told me so often how good human flesh was I made up my mind to taste it.

On Sunday June 3, 1928, I called on you at 406 W 15 Street. Brought you pot cheese- strawberries. We had lunch. Grace sat on my lap and kissed me. I made up my mind to eat her on the pretense of taking her to a party. You said yes she could go.

I took her to an empty house in Westchester I had already picked out. When we got there, I told her to remain outside. She picked wildflowers. I went upstairs and stripped all my clothes off. I knew if I did not I would get her blood on them. When all was ready I went to the window and called her. Then I hid in a closet until she was in the room.

When she saw me all naked she began to cry and tried to run downstairs. I grabbed her and she said she would tell her mamma. First I stripped her naked. How she did kick- bite and scratch. I choked her to death, then cut her in small pieces so I could take her meat to my rooms, cook and eat it.

How sweet and tender her little ass was roasted in the oven. It took me 9 days to eat her entire body. I did not fuck her tho I could of had I wished. She died a virgin.

49

Grace Budd's Kidnaper-Slayer Leads Police to Child's '28 Grave

Associated Press photos

Albert H. Fish leaving Police Headquarters yesterday. Inset, Grace Budd

Mild-Mannered Father of Six, 65, Trapped by Letters Written to Girl's Parents, Admits Butchering; Victim's Head Found in Westchester

New York Herald Tribune - December 14, 1931

Fish's Own Story Of 'Weird Life'

THE DAILY MIRROR herewith presents the life story of Albert H. Fish, as fantastic a figure of a man as ever went on trial for murder. There is no thought of in any way prejudicing either the prosecution or the defense, or of passing judgment on whether Fish is legally sane. This material is given as a psychological exhibit.

By *A. H. Fish*

I am a man of passion. You don't know what that means, unless you are my kind. At the orphanage where they put me just before Garfield was assassinated, there were some older boys that caught a horse in a sloping field.

"Fish says, 'I am a man of passion. You don't know what that means unless you are my kind.' Fish never spoke a truer word. It is not physical passion that Fish speaks of. It is that Fish has developed conflicting impulses. If properly examined one would find that one part of his personality dominates entirely over the other part. At one time Fish will remember all past events with an indescribable vividness. At another time the events of his life are completely blotted out and he is living the life of an entirely different person in his consciousness."
Dr. Edward Spencer Cowles, Famous Psychiatrist, New York Daily Mirror—March 13, 1935

51

The following was ran in the New York Daily Mirror Newspaper beginning March 12, 1935.

FISH'S OWN STORY OF "WEIRD LIFE"
By A.H. Fish

I am a man of passion. You don't know what that means, unless you are my kind. At the orphanage where they put me just before Garfield was assassinated, there were some older boys that caught a horse in a sloping field.

They got the horse up against a fence down at the bottom of the field and tied him up. An old horse. They put kerosene on his tail and litit and cut the rope and away went that old horse busting through fences to get away from the fire. But the fire went with him.

That horse, that's me. That's the man of passion. The fire chases you and catches you and then it's in your blood. And after that, it's the fire that has control, not the man. Blame the fire of passion for what Albert H. Fish has done.

What has Albert H. Fish done? Sometimes I, myself, am not sure what is real and what is not; what I've really done and what are things I wanted to do and thought about doing, so long that it got to be as if I had done them so that I "remember" them just as clearly as the real things, just as clearly as that hot Sunday in June when I went to the window and whistled to that little grace Budd and she stopped picking daisies and came in.

THERE ARE A LOT OF US

But some of the other things are just as real. Though I can see that people don't believe me when I tell about them. That makes me mad. I mean, not being believed makes me mad. What's the matter with these people? Don't they want to believe the truth about me? Do they just want to close their eyes and ears and make believe to themselves that the sort of thing I can tell about, doesn't exist? Well, it does. And plenty. There are lots of us. We know how to find each other out and get together and have fun.

We use the matrimonial agencies and the want ads and there are hundreds of other ways. We have our own language, a sort of code. I'll tell all about that when I get to it.

But what I want to make clear at the start, is that I'll put down the things I know to be true. Things I actually did. When I put down something that was imagined and not carried out, I'll come right out and say so. I'll say: "Now that's one of the things I thought about doing, but never got around to doing it. Principally because some ideas you get if you are a man of passion are so hard to carry out that you never get around to it and here I am 65 years old and in jail, so it looks like they'll have to be dropped after all."

And if they insist that some of these things, the biggest things I've ever done, are imaginings, why, I can answer them with:

If I am being tried for the murder of that little girl, certainly that was not imagining, was it? And if that really happened, why not the others?

MARRIAGE SERVES ONE PURPOSE

The thing that started me on the real big things I have done in the last fifteen years, was the trouble I had in 1917 with my wife and that man John Straub. Marriage is not all that it is cracked up to be, but it certainly serves one purpose. So long as the man and woman keep the bargain, they will both stay out of other trouble. It is a good safety valve. As long as Anna stuck to me and the children kept coming one after the other until there were six, I might have my outside fancies, but would keep my end of the bargain and fancies they would stay, nothing more.

But when the dog sniffed at the attic door, and I found Straub lying up there waiting for my wife to bring him the cuts she sneaked from the family table, my eyes were opened to the fact that no bargain holds and that only fools know any restraints. That freed me. It threw off my chains. I had a right after that to any fun I could find or grab.

We were living then in a house at No. 1013 Fifth Ave., College Point, the eight of us, Anna and myself and the six children, headed by Albert, who was 18 and had a job at the John W. Rapp Works at 10th Ave. and 3rd St., College Point. We were getting along fine. I have always been pretty good at my trade of house painting and we set a good table and paid the rent.

We had a small dog, and it was always my custom to keep a pretty good track of income and outgo. Put it all down, I say, and you'll never be fooled. I kept track in a little book I carried with me, not only of the money, but of food and clothing and all. And my book showed me about the time that we were using up more food than I saw going down anybody's throat. I asked Anna:

"What's become of all this food? The way I figure it, there's about ten pounds of meat a week and other stuff over and above what I can check."

TOO MUCH FOOD EATEN

If I had any suspicions, I would have noticed how she got confused when she passed it off by saying that the dog was eating his head off. That drew my attention to the dog, which was just a cur the children had picked up. I wondered how such a small dog could get away with so much food. I figured it out he must be cacheing the food the way animals do.

I set a watch and one evening I saw that dog start up the stairs and I followed him. The dog went on up to a door leading into a kind of attic store-room and began sniffing and whining at the crack. I thought to myself now I've found the place where you cache all that stuff and what a mess that will be.

I opened the attic door and went in. It was a bit dark in there and I stumbled over a heap on the floor. It was this Straub, sound asleep on the floor, snug as a bug in a rug in a spread of some of the best blankets and quilts in the house. He sat up half asleep and mumbled something about: "What have you got for me this time?"
I have always liked things to be easy and pleasant around me. Men of my type are like

that. Even those I have handled rough, I would like it if they liked it too, if you know what I mean. If only pain were not so painful.

But my main thought was that this might be excitement, something new: live and let live. It was pretty funny leading Straub downstairs and walking into the dining room and telling him to pull up a chair. He was struck dumb. So was my wife. They didn't know what was coming next. Neither did I.

CHAPTER II

If I had any definite idea in mind at all when I fetched Anna's lover down from the attic and made him sit at the table across from me, with Anna between, it was certainly no idea of violence.

That came after, when he and Anna sold the furniture to a junk man and left me the six children and took a honeymoon in Bridgeport on the money. That was going too far.

After a couple have been married nineteen years and have brought up six children, I think it must be the rule that early passion is pretty well petered out. Why not be frank about it? If the vitality peters out with the passion, everything comes out all right at the end, and the old folks sit around getting their fun, if any, out of crossword puzzles and a pack of cards. But the trouble is that the vitality doesn't always peter out at the right time, and why not be frank about this too?

There are thousands, probably millions, of old people going around who have been stuck up on the shelf and are too lively to stay there. When I got looking around in the last few years, hunting for my own kind, why I found that the world is simply littered with people of both sexes on the wrong side of fifty according to the calendar, but still twenty and full of Old Nick in their minds.
"Read this."

"Mo 520- lonely widow, would be a companion to some young old man. Love home and would do all in my power to make some man happy. Want a man with a loving disposition. Considered very nice looking for a lady of my age which is 60. Have dark brown hair and dark gray eyes, 5-5, 180 lbs. Very friendly and sociable. Have some property."

That is an ad from one of the matrimonial magazines. I know all about these lonely widows. I married three of them in 1930. One was all right and her daughter even better, as I shall tell when I get to the story of my adventure with Myrna and Mary of Ohio.

But the best that can be said for the matrimonial agencies is that the contacts they provide are better than nothing, better than sitting in the rocker and waiting for the undertaker, but the old don't want the old. The desire for youth and beauty does not get less with time, but greater and greater as the years go by. What to do? I must have found the wrong answer.

ANGER AGAINST HIS WIFE

All this is meant to explain how I felt, discovering that my wife of nineteen years, mother of my six children, was keeping this fellow, Straub, in the attic. It wasn't anger I felt. It was envy. The anger came later when she did the really disloyal thing, walked out on our bargain, which was to do the fair thing by our children, and left me to shoulder that burden alone.

A few days after I had heaped coals of fire on Straub's head by putting him at my table, he vanished, and then I myself left the home in College Point to go out on a job.

A housepainter usually moves in on his job. I was a good one and building and remodeling was booming and that meant I was away from home more than I was in it. My custom was to leave my forwarding address with my eldest daughter named Anna after her mother, and who is Mrs. Anna Collings now and lives in Astoria.

Fish Continues His Weird Story

TOLD WIFE WAS GONE

The job was an interior decorating one in White Plains, the same town where I face a murder trial now, a bad place for me. The weather was bitter cold that Winter and this was the middle of January. I got daughter Anna's telegram on Jan. 19, 1917, at 12 Brookfield St., White Plains, which is in the colored district now, but was a white rooming house section then. The telegram said: "Papa, Mama is gone. Come home, Anna"

I put two and two together and knew instantly that she had run off with Straub, but it wasn't until I got to College Point that night that I knew the whole damage she had done when I went into the house. The first thing that struck me was that the hall tree had been moved.

A neighbor woman met me in the hall and said: "She's gone, Mr. Fish, and everything you had is gone with her."

I heard the children crying in the dining room and went in. The room was absolutely bare. Even the stove was gone. Along with a three-leaf maple table and twelve chairs of a set and the sideboard and rug.

Because of the icy cold, the children were all huddled together at the street window in their hats and coats and I got the story from them all.

"Mama gave us all a dime and sent us to the movies at 4 o' clock," they all screamed.

"Ten minutes after they all left for the movies, a van that was waiting down the street moved up to the door and John Straub showed up," a neighbor said. "The van men and Straub moved every stick out of the house and drove off and then your wife left too."

"I rushed through the place like a blind man. It was like being struck blind, seeing nothing where there had been a home. The beds and even the bed clothing were gone, so that in pure pity, like after a fire or a shipwreck or something, the neighbors had to take us in for the night to keep warm and have time to think what to do next.

HOME POSSESSIONS SOLD, HE SAYS

The next day, I found out that the van, everything I possessed in the world, had been sold by Anna for next to nothing, to the first second-hand man she had found. It was enough to get her and her lover over the State line to Bridgeport, Conn.

I had to rent a furnished flat by the week. I remember the landlady took one look at my string of children and boosted the rent to $25 a week and also made me pay $10 down on breakage.

We left that place two weeks later. I had to make a complete new start in life as mother and father of six mouths, but I never got that $10 back, even though one glass was all we broke all the time we were there.

Well, trouble for one is profit for two. My eldest son, Albert, was working for a foreman named William Konzet, who used to visit us at times. Konzet looked me up. He was angrier about the whole affair than I was.

I was too stunned to feel rage. Konzet told me I could get Straub on the Mann Act and at least get back the money value of what had been stolen.

TRACED WIFE TO BRIDGEPOST

I traced Anna and Straub to a rooming house at 21 Harrison St., Bridgeport, and got a policeman, but when we crashed in, the birds had flown.

I heard from Anna once about three years later. My three youngest children had come down with the measles and I was at my wits end. She heard about this in some round-about way and wrote to daughter Anna:

"Straub can't get a job and your mother is literally starving up here with her two new babies. I've heard about Gene and Gert and Johnny having the measles and if your father isn't too mad at me, I would come back simply as a housekeeper and work for my keep and work hard. Only one thing you are to tell him. If he takes me in, I have to bring these two babies with me. But not Straub."

Anna sounded me out on the letter but I had had enough, and said so. Straub I ran into just once a few years later, when I was working on a building about a mile away and I went over there and saw an unfurnished two-story house and Straub carrying a stack of shingles up an outside ladder.

I went after him. He saw me coming and ducked in a window on the second floor. I went in after him and saw a finished flight of stairs ahead and went on up full speed.

PERSUED STRAUB

What I did not know was that there was a piece of closet space to the one side of the stairs and that Straub had died in there to hide while I rushed by. I was going so fast, when I got to the top that I pitched over the edge of nothing and barely saved myself from a nasty fall by hugging an upright as I went over.

Straub slipped down inside the house and out the back while I was climbing back to safety and left the job and that part of the world.

Over in Astoria where he and Anna live now, he must be one of those who figure that the worst the jury can do to me here is all to the good. I can only hope and pray that my faithless wife does not share that feeling against the husband whose only offense against her is that she did him wrong.

Children are solace for somethings and I cherish and have cherished my own, every one. But they are not solace for the loneliness that strikes a man when fate tells him that his pleasures in life are over. I was driven in on myself in those years, years after the earthquake that demolished my home. That was when I began to write the letters. I was visited by peculiar dreams that got me through the nights. The letters continued those dreams through the days.

CHAPTER III

"Dear Miss-(The name does not matter. I got it from a nurses' registry.)

"I am a widower of some means. A stock broker in Standard Oil of New Jersey. I am sixty-five years of age and in very feeble health. I have a son of nineteen. He is a semi-invalid.

When five years of age, he fell down the cellar stairs. Sustained a brain concussion. When twelve, he had a sever attack of infantile paralysis: he cannot walk, run, jump, get in and out of bathtub without assistance.

There is no lifting to do or a wheel chair to push. However, Bobby has very little use of his arms and hands. He has to be washed, dressed, undressed, given a bath and rubbed all over daily with alcohol. He has had one young woman in charge of him for the past seven years, Miss Helen Brown, she is leaving because of her coming marriage. Now, though Bobby is going on 20, is good looking, well built and weighs 165 pounds, he is just as easy to spank or switch as a boy of ten. Frequently, he gets cranky and does not mind."

GOOD TIMES, GOOD PAY FOR GOOD SERVICE

"Miss Brown has a paddle and cat o' nine tails. On such occasions, she did not hesitate to use one or both on his quite freely, in fact, that is the only way you can handle him. I want a young woman, not a mere girl. Who can and will take full charge of him. There is no woman in the house to butt in. You will be entirely his boss and mine as well.

When he doesn't mind, do exactly as Miss Brown did and go as far as you like. Don't be stingy. If I don't take my medicine or mind you, give me the same as you do the boy.

It is not a question of money. Good pay-good times-for good service."
(Signed) "Albert H. Fish"

FOUND A CODE TO SOUND PEOPLE

This letter I have copied in here is one of the kind I got in the habit of writing after my wife left me alone to brood and face old age alone. Of course, it is not the kind

I wrote to myself, not the kind I wrote to lots of people, principally women, after I had sounded them out and found out that their ideas ran along the same as mine.

Those other letters are freer and say exactly what was on my mind. But I understand they cannot be printed which is too bad. There would be lots less trouble int eh world, lots less of people keeping the lid on until they pop. If you could write and print things just as they come to mind- one free spirit talking to another free spirit. And I found lots of free spirits to talk with and write to after I got the hang of things and looked around.

But this letter illustrates something I wrote awhile back about my kind having a way to find each other out, a kind of code.

I found out, after I had been in trouble a couple of times, that in this letter writing business you have to sound people out before you let go and write what you want. This letter is a "sounding out-" letter. I might call it good old Number One.

Now it is full of code. All that about the alcohol rubs and the cat-o'-nine-tails and "good pay and good times," that's all code. If the party understands and answers in the same code then everything is clear sailing. And the beauty of it is that if the party misunderstands and writes back about some real professional nursing, no harm is done. You just write back and say, sorry, the job is filled.

AND THEN BOBBY GOT TO BE REAL

"Bobby" was my own special invention. I have no son named Bobby who is an invalid. But you can't come right out in the first letter and say that Bobby is yourself; that you are the one that needs to be handled like a spoiled child and switched. Some people would think it was silly. Some would think worse.

But "Bobby" got to be more than a code word to me. He got to be real some times. He drove me into a fury. Having to be babied and tended night and day and by me who had six other real children on my hands. A big blubbering lout of a fellow, though handsome and well formed, it drove me to violence to be saddled with his care.

Then out would come the whip and strap and he would get what for. I believe those beatings I experienced were the origin of the habit I contracted later on of sticking needles into myself. The trouble with pain is you get tough and always have to invent something that hurts worse.

I a curious way, too, "Bobby" was somebody else, neither me nor a code figure, but a person long dead, Albert H. Fish. Now, don't jump. I'm not suggesting that I myself was long dead. But Albert H. Fish did die at the age of 18 months in Washington, D. C., in 1865.

TAKES NAME OF DEAD BROTHER

Mark Twain has a funny story about a pair of twins which sort of applies in my case. The Twain story is told by the surviving twin of a pair, one of which died in the cradle without the nurse exactly knowing which of the two it was had died. And the story ends up with the living twin saying "the twin who died was me."

I was not baptized Albert H. Fish. Before I was born, the 19th of May, 1870 in

Washington, D.C., my parents had another boy who had been baptized by that name just before he died from having been born with water on the brain. The doctor int hat case and one who brought me into the world was a famous Washington doctor, by the way, Dr. Robert Rayburn, one of the two specialists who later attended President Garfield on his death bed when he was shot, and later got big Congressional grants as fees.

Well, Albert H. Fish died in the cradle, and later I came along and was baptized with a name that got me called insulting nicknames in the orphanage where I lived three years of early childhood and learned most of the things which developed into some of my unusual habits later on. The nicknames were unbearable. When my mother got going again after my fathers death and took me out of the orphanage and I was to go to public school, I told her all about the nicknames and begged her to give me a new name.

I remember how she looked at me and patted my hand and sat me in her apron and said:

"You can have the name of your baby brother you never saw, Albert. Anyway, getting you back from the orphanage was like getting my son back from the dead."

CHAPTER IV

Sometimes I think there is no such thing as time. My childhood seems yesterday. And yesterday seems long ago. You will have to follow me if I jump back and forth from century to century. I'm old enough to have done a lot of living in two.

What I want to tell now is partly in 1875, partly in 1931, just the other day in the Steeplechase Hotel at Rockaway Beach, where I got into that trouble from tossing over the wall of that high-class girls' school.

There was a connection between my childhood and that trouble about the girls' school, you see. I also had been shut up in an orphanage and I knew just how those girls felt being shut up in those finishing school grounds with all their temperament going to waste.

People who run schools and orphanages don't know what they are doing when they try to keep the lid on the boys and girls under them. I do. The orphanage people were very strict. They kept the boys and girls separate and of course all we thought of then was how to get together. The higher-ups never found out about those loose planks in the dormitory floor.

LEARNED TO LIE AND STEAL

That sort of thing went on under cover while the praying and the learning went on in the open. It was like living two lives, one they knew about, one they didn't. And also, I learned at that orphanage to beg, lie and steal.

Here was how I learned to beg: The orphanage was a charity place and their biggest expense was feeding the herd. They used to dress us up in a kind of uniform and give us each a big cloth bag. The bag had painted on it in big letters: "FILL ME UP."

We went into grocery stores and meat markets and stood near the door and spread out the bag so the begging words showed and then we folded our hands and looked like praying, until the owner saw that the customers expected it of him and filled the bag.

And here was how I learned to steal and lie: The orphanage sent out the bigger boys with tin boxes with slits in the top for dropping coins, from pennies to half-dollars.

The last year I was there, I was sent out with a bigger boy to learn. We went to the right places and the box got filled and then, on the way back, the bigger boy took me up an alley and showed me a strip of tin he had hidden in his stocking and how to use it by poking it into the half-dollar slot and letting the money slide out along it.

I got rehearsed also in how to tell the orphanage heads a long story about how people weren't giving quarters and halves any more, but dimes at the most. So I was as good as a thief and liar as the rest and they let me on the tin-box pool.

So it was really memories of all that had happened to me when I was behind walls, too, that drove me to toss those letters over the wall of the girls' school near Rockaway Beach. They were not the plainest letters I can write, either, but just written for fun to make the girls laugh.

But the headmistress got one of them and complained to the detective, John P. Smith of the 100th Precinct in Rockaway and they came up and got me at the Steeple-chase Hotel, where I had a job as a dishwasher and a back room in the staff wing.

That was the second time I was taken to a hospital for observation. I was taken to Bellevue in 1930 and the doctors there said I was harmless. This time I was taken to Kings County by Dr. Louis Berlatt of Rockaway Beach Hospital. But they let me go again.

And I think that this is what will happen a third time at the end of this trial of mine for putting that little Budd girl out of the way.

"If Fish's story, that he came suddenly upon his wife's lover in the attic of his home (and even though he possessed sufficient self-control to invite him to dinner with his wife, Anna, and himself) is correct, it is highly probable that he sustained a psychic trauma; that the shock of the incident weakened the controlling forces in his brain. The wife, Anna, and her lover selling the furniture, sneaking away, leaving the children in the cold, base rooms, the responsibility of Fish, unleashed the murderous impulses of his submerged personality."
- Dr. Edward Cowles

"Pop never lifted a hand to any of us. He even scolded my sister Anna when she punished her youngsters. It doesn't seem possible that he could have murdered the little Budd girl, because he was always so kind to us while my mother, when they were still living together, was always looking out for herself. When they separated, twenty years ago, it was Pop who held the family together."
- Gertrude DeMarco, Fish's Daughter

Albert Fish and Detective William King.

#1

Page 174 - Par 570-1-2
Showing bones to Jury
" " Skull " "
Plainly done to create animosity in their
minds
Show authority of the D-A. to show such
evidence. Never done in Court before.

Page 175 Par 573 - 575
Court answers full responsibility.
Ask for mistrial - motion denied.
No reason for showing skull and bones
to establish fact - when they had doctors
to prove that beyond a doubt
They had for Spines

Defendant looks as to June 3 - 1925 - to
Dec 13 - 34. Same style of hat- manner of
dress. Same small mustache. No attempt
to hide or disguise. Working in many
places about city.

64

Wel. to J.W. Jr.
Sept 27/1935
Death House

Page 174 - Par 520-1-2
Showing bones to Jury
    "   skull   "

Plainly done to create animosity in their minds.
Show authority of the D.A. to show such evidence. Never been done in Court before.

Page 175 Par 573-575
Court assures full responsibility.
Ask for mistrial - motion denied.
No reason for showing skull and bones to establish fact- when they had doctors to prove that- beyond a doubt
they had Dr Squins.

Defendant looks as to June 3- 1928- to Dec 13- 34. Same style of hat- manner of dress. Same small mustache. No attempt to hide or disguise. Working in many places about city.

Page 192 Par.

Letter to Mrs Budd Nov 11-34.
Wm F. King admits def spoke in secret
of stories told def- by his brother a sailor
of famine in china. children sold by
parents-to be used as flesh and eaten in
order to preserve life in others. def in Home
from age of 5 to 7. Saw all kinds of immoral
acts- by older boys and girls- learned to do the
same. Locked out spanked for least thing.
Learned to lie- by- steal. After leaving
home- went to School. Made fun of and
mocked- changed name at age of 15. Brother
told all kinds of stories. Sailors caught
by savages- stripped naked- roasted- eaten
Def- believed same- was much impressed.
Great reader of Bible and refers to follows-
Genesis chap 6- 6-11-12-13 Verse. Genesis chap
21- 2-3-4-22 Verse. Genesis chap 22- 1-2-3-6-
9-10-11-12 Verse. Genesis chap 39- 7-8-9-10-11-12
Verse. Numbers chap 11- 6-11-12-13-14-15- Verse.
Deut chap 21- 18-19-20-21 Verse. Deut 23 chap
1-2-13-17- Verse. Joshua chap 5- 2 Verse. Isaiah
chap 36- 12- Verse. Jeremiah chap 19-9- Verse
the Acts chap 16- 17-19- 22- Verse.

Page 192 Par.

Letter to Mrs. Budd Nov 11- 34

Wm. F. King admits def - spoke in same of stories told Def.- by his brother a sailor of famine in China. Children sold by parents - to be used as flesh and eaten in order to preserve life in others. Def in Home from age of 5 to 7. Saw all kinds of immoral acts - by older boys and girls - learned to do the same. Lashed out and spanked for leart thing. Learned to lie - beg - steal. After leaving home - went to school. Main form of acct never - changed same at age of 15. Brother told all kinds of stories. Sailors caught by savages - stripped naked - roasted - eaten Def believed same- was most impressed. Great reader of Bible and refers to follows- Genesis Chap 6 = 6- 11- 12- 13 verse. Genesis Chap 22= 1- 2- 3- 6- 9- 10- 11- 12 verse. Genesis Chap 39 = 7- 8- 9- 10- 11- 12 verse. Numbers Chap 11= 6- 11- 12- 13- 14- 5- verse. Deut Chap 21= 18- 19- 20- 21 verse. Deut 23 Chap 1- 2- 3- 7- verse. Joshua chap 5= 2 verse. Isiaih chap 36= 12- verse. Jeremiah Chap 19- 9- verse The Acts Chap 16= 17- 19- 22 verse.

At age of ten began to read daily Papers. Read out in the Evening Star. Leading evening paper published in Washin D.C. Admiral Perrys expt. to North Pole financed by N.S. Gritt food supply exausted. 3 of crew cooked and eaten before rescue party arrived. Always had desire to find out just what human flesh cooked in various ways tasted likl. Was interested in TORTURE of any kind. Looked for books bearing on same. found just what I wanted in Quo Vadis Neros tort are of the Christians. Guy Fawlks Spanish Inquisition Mary Queen of Scotts who bathed in the blood of small children rone drn 12. Chinese Pirates Coopers Indian Tales. Always had strong desire to read out in daily Papers of any one being tarred and feathered. she colored by of 16. I had an the old boat in Washin D.C. had 4 Aunts. One of these lived at Falls church Va. She had a white man boarding with her. He raped her 15 yr old girl. She and 5 other colored women took him out of bed. stripped off his night shirt Tied him to a tree and all of these dashed his bare behind till he bled

#3

At age of ten began to read Daily Papers. Read acct in The Evening Star. Leading eve paper published in Washin D.C. Admiral Perrys expd - to North Pole financed by U.S. Gov't. Food supply exhausted - 3 of crew - cooked and eaten before rescue party arrived. Always had desire to find out just what human flesh - cooked in various ways - tasted like. Was interested in TORTURE of - any - kind. Looked for books - bearing on same. Found just what I wanted in 3 Quo Vadis Neros torture of the Christians. Guy Fawlkes - Spanish Inquisition - Mary - Queen of Scots- who bathed in the blood of small children- none over 12. Chinese Pirates - Coopers Indian Tales. Always had strong desire to read acct in the Daily Papers of any one being tarred and feathered. The colored boy of 16 - I had on the old boat in Washin D.C. had 2 Aunts. One of them lived at Falls Church VA. She had a white man boarding with her. He raped her 15 year old girl. She and 5 other - colored women took him out of bed - stripped off his night shirt. Tied him to a tree and all of them lashed his bare behind - till he bled.

Having no tar - they spilled a gallon of black molasses over him - ripped open a pillow and dumped the feathers all over him. James told me this many times and both of us said how we would of liked to have been there. To hear him scream when being switched and seen him how funny he must have looked - like a human chicken. I got a thrill every time I read of a nigger who had raped a white girl in the South and he was taken from the Police. He was stripped - Castrated - emasculated. Oil was then poured over him and set on fire. It thrilled me greatly when I read of the two men who were Lynched out in California 2 years ago. I read it in several papers. The mob that got Holmes was led by a pretty blond girl of 17. She helped to men - sting - him - tore - roped and he was marched from the jail to the tree - in that state there the crowd swung him to air naked a. 1500 men - women - boys - girls looked on and cheered. When I was in the home I made up my mind if I ever got the chance to do so. I would whip and torture children for the pleasure of hearing them scream as I

#4

Having no tar - they spilled a gallon of black molasses on him- ripped open a pillow and dumped the feathers all on him. James told me this many times and both of us said how we would liked to have been there. To hear him scream when being switched and seen him how funny he must have looked - like a human chicken. I got a thrill - every time when I read of a nigger who had raped a white girl in the South and he was taken from the Police. He was stripped - castrated - emasculated. Oil was then poured on him and set on fire. It thrilled me greatly when I read of the two men who were lynched out in California 2 years ago. I read it in several papers. The mob that got Halvces was led by a pretty blond girl of 17. She helped men - strip - him - bare - naked and he was marched from the jail to the tree - in that state - thru the crowd. Strung up in the air naked as 1500 men - women - boys - girls - looked on and cheered. When I was in the home I made up my mind - if I ever got the chance to do so. I would whip and torture children for the pleasure of hearing them scream as I

have been made sexual. The first chance I
got was with this colored boy and ever since
I have never missed a chance to do so. I had
laid in bed with many boys from 12 to 17.
The first <u>man</u> who ever had me was the one
I met in N.J. City. He took me to 95 Bowery
a Lodging House. I was <u>3 nights with him</u>.
He is also the first <u>man</u> I ever sucked off.
tho I had done it with many boys & girls.

Page ~~595~~ 195 - Par 584 - Wm F. King tells you that
I had in mind - a boy - always I had a boy
in mind. I wanted to <u>castigate him</u>
just to see <u>what he looked like</u> that day
and of course <u>hear him scream</u> - when
<u>I cut it off</u>. K- admits I had the boy in
mind and that I intended to castigate him
and kill him. I knew a boy of 18 had some
meat on his behind that I could cook and
eat. I can think of no reason why I took the
girl. knew she existed but had never seen
her <u>prior</u> to June 3 - 1928. When she sat in my
lap the divine command to see that she
died a Virgin came over me and I took her.
for her parents <u>refused</u>. she used to kiss then home

#5

have been made scream. The first chance I got was with this colored boy and ever since I have never missed a chance to do so. I had laid in bed with many boys from 12 to 17. The first man who ever had me was the one I met in N.Y. City. He took me to 95 Bowery a Lodging House. I was 3 nights with him. He is also the first man I ever sucked off. Tho I had done it - with many boys & girls.

Page 583 195 - Par 584 = Wm. F. King tells you that I had in mind - a boy - always I had a boy in mind. I wanted to castigate him just to see what he looked like that way. And of course hear him scream - when I cut it off. K - admits I had the boy in mind and that I intended to castigate him and kill him. I knew a boy of 18 had some meat on his behind - that I could cook and eat. I can think of no reason why I took the girl. Knew she existed but have never seen her - prior to June 3 - 1928. When she got in my lap the Devine Command to see that she died a Virgin came on me and I took her. Had her parents refused - she would be in their home.

Prior to the Budd case — I had met Cyril Quinn
several times. First in 1921 at 1444 Park ave.
He was living there with his father & brothers.
I was also living there. He came up to my
room. One Sunday when I was all alone.
Asked me if he could look at the funny papers.
I said yes come in — while he was doing so
I stripped naked and remained so for the
entire time he was in my room. Going
back and forth in front of him — so he could
see me nude. He told other boys and when they
knew I was alone — several came in to see
me naked. We had all kinds of relations as
well as spanking each other. I moved to
222 E 70 st and Cyril to 225 E 70. He came
to my rooms and brought other boys. All of us
stripped naked — spanked each other — done it.
It was at 222 E 70 I met the boy whose father
send me wood coal — wood ice. The boy
most always brought it. When I ordered 25¢ worth
of wood I stripped naked. In a few minutes
the boy came. When he knocked I said Come in
He could hardly keep the wood from Looking
at me. He took as long as he could — went
out. then knocked again and said — can I

#6

Prior to the Budd case- I had met Cyril Quinn several times. First in 1921 at 1444 Park Ave. He was living there with his father & brother. I was also living there. He came up to my room one Sunday when I was all alone. Asked me if he could look at the funny papers. I said yes come in - while he was doing so I stripped naked and remained so for the entire time he was in my room. Going back in forth in front of him - so he could see-me-good. He told other boys and when they knew - I was alone - several came in - to see me naked. We had all kinds of relations as well as spanking each other. I moved to 222 E 70 St and Cyril to 225 E 70. He came to my rooms and brought other boys. All of us stripped naked - spanked each other - done it. It was at 222 E 70 I met the boy whose father served me with coal - wood - ice. The boy most always brought it. When I ordered 25¢ worth of wood I stripped naked. In a few minutes the boy came. When he knocked - I said come in He could hardly carry the wood from Looking at me. He took as long as he could - went out - then knocked again and said - can I

has a drink of water. I said sure - come in
and get it. I could see he liked what he saw
so I walked across the floor - turning back
and front to him - so he could see - all I had.
That was Sat - same night he met Gil Quinn
and said he saw me 'all bare' and spoke of the
big monkey - I had. Sunday I had them both -
they had me. When I moved to 40 9 E 100 I sent
Gil a letter and told him to come up & bring
Tony. I had some time prior to this - bought
the tools spoke of. I intended to kill both of
them. Cut off their Penis - split it open - broil
it on the gas and eat it as well as their
nice fat behinds - and meat off their belly
and legs. Both were on the bed - bare naked
for some reason - Gil raised one end of the
mattress - saw the tools and got scared. I
never saw him or Tony again.

Page 226 Par 677 - 8 - 9 -
Looks same as did June 3 - 1928
Subject of marriages 3 in 1930 - all of them
within a period of a few months. Never
got a dime or stood long enough with any
one of the 3 - to really know them.

#7

have a drink of water. I said sure - come in and get it. I could see he like what he saw so I walked across the floor - turning back and front - to him - so he could see - all-I-had. That was Sat - same night - he met Cyril Quinn and said he saw me 'all bare' and spoke of the big monkey- I had. Sunday I had them both - they had me. When I moved to 409 E 100 I sent Cyril a letter and told him to come up & bring Tony. I had some time prior to this - bought the tools spoke of. I intended to kill - both of them. Cut off their Penis - split it open - broil it on the gas and eat it as well as their nice fat behinds and meat off their belly and legs. Both were on the bed - bare naked for some reason - Cyril raised one end of the mattress - sees the tools and got scared. I never sees him or Tony again.

Page 226 Par 677- 8- 9-
Looks same as did June 3- 1928
Subject of marriages 3 in 1930 - all of them within a period of four months. Never got a divorce or staid long enough with any one of the 3- to really know them.

the knowing nothing of law I noticed in
court that in most cases on material
points the ~~Judge~~ favored the D.A. — as
against council for defence. My being
somewhat deaf prevented me hearing
all. On the whole tho I can — see. Note
Page 245 — Par 734 — I note a number of times
where the D.A. accused you of — Leading —
putting the answer in the mouth of wit
on stand. In my case he was upheld
by the Judge. I also note several occasions
where Judge accuses you of making a speech
I have never read of such before at any
1st dg murder trials where a mans life
is at stake. Here is one point I would like
to have you impress upon the mind of the
Judges of the Court of appeals. Had I not got
answers from many of those I wrote to.
Who agreed to do just what I wished. there
nothing urged on I might of dropped dead.
One of the most striking is Mrs B. Kukon
claremont N.Y. She has a girl of 15 and Mr
Pell or A. H. F. was to N spanked — snatched
from a birth and kept in his room to
about the house — Naked for a Month. You

#8

tho knowing nothing of Law I noticed in court - that in most cases on material points - the Judge favored the DA - as against the council for defence. My being somewhat deaf prevented me hearing all. For the record tho I can - see. Note Page 245 - Par 734 - I note a number of times where the D.A. accused you of - Leading - putting the answer in the mouth of wit on stand. In every case he was upheld by the Judge. I also note several occasions where the Judge accuses you of - making a speech I have never read of such before at any 1st deg murder trial - where a man's life is at stake. Here is one point I would like to have you impress before the mind of the Judge of the Court of Appeals. Had I not got answers from many of those I wrote to. Who agreed to do just what I wished. Then not being urged on I might of dropped out. One of the most stricking is Mrs. B. Kukon Claremont N.Y. she has a girl of 15 and Mr. Pell - or A.H.F was to be spanked - scratched given a bath and kept in his room to about the house - Naked for a month. You

NEW YORK, FRIDAY, DECEMBER 14, 1934.

Budd Girl's Body Found; Killed by Painter in 1928

Slayer, Trapped After Sending Letters to Family, Admits Abducting Child, 10 — Leads Way to Westchester Grave.

89

have some of her letters. They speak for themselves same as my own to. Take a few along with you when you go to Albany.

I note on pages 520-1 you move to have the indictment set aside on the ground the People have not proved a Prima-facia Case. I have read Testimony of Doctors for and against me. I find the same procedure all thru. Where a point was in my favor it was stricken out. Where it was in favor of the D.A. he was upheld. I think in view of the Rating your Drs have as against the other side and the any apparent partiality shown the D.A. you have an excellent case for a reversal. If you recall during the trial I spoke to you of how Judge Case seemed to me - to rule against you - where he could. Then again the Judges can note the difference in time of my 'exam'. Dr. Wertham Dr Jelliffe Dr Riley spent 24 hours. Other side 6·1/4 and 3 of that was by a man whom I saw in the Tombs hand out Pills and weigh medicine. You should have asked for his disqualification as an expert.

86

have some of her letters - they speak for themselves same as my own do. Take a few along with you when you go to Albany.

I note on pages 520-1 you move to have the indictment set aside on the ground the People have not proved a Prima - Facia - Case. I have read Testimony of Doctors for and against me. I find the same procedure all three. Where a point was in my favor it was stricken out. When it was in favor of the D.A. he was upheld. I think in view of the Rating your Drs have - against the other side and the very apparent partiality shown the D.A. you have an excellent case for a reversal. If you recall - during the trial I spoke to you of how Judge Close seemed to me - to rule against you - when he could. Then again the Judges can note the difference in tone of my 'excuses.' Dr Wertham- Dr Jellip - Dr Riley spent 24 hours. Other side 6 1/4 and 3 of that was by a man whom I saw in the Tombs hand out Pills and cough medicine. You should have asked for his disqualifications as expert.

#10

Be sure and stress that items and the dif-
ine time print by both sides. Also stress
what a shock I got Jan 19-1917- when
I came home and found an empty
house - my 6 children homeless as well
as Motherless - all in one night. Stress
that I have never been the same man since.

That is a good point you take on Page 656
Par 1967 about the Warden- stress it
That is also a good point on Page 754 Par
2262 - Drive it home. Page 657 Par 2264
I am sure now of a re-versal.
Page 878 Par 2633 = shows mind of Judge.
Page 983 Par 2947-48- there you hit back.
Any one not an idiot could see how one
sided the whole trial was. The Court
of Appeals are not included. Now I am
going to sum up. All six of my children
1 grand child - 1 step child have testified
in my behalf. They went thru a lot of
misery and what did they accomplish?
Absolutely nothing. The d.a. has last word
and that - counts. He said - you know
blood is thicker than water. There is no
    Ask for change of Venue - N.Y. or Queens Co

88

#10

Be sure and stress that item and the dif- in fine spent by both sides. Also stress what a shock I got Jan 19- 1917 - when I came home and found an empty house - my 6 children homeless as well as motherless - all in one night. Stress that I have never been the same man since.

That is a good point you take on Page 656 Par 1967 about the Warden - stress it. That is also a good poin on Page 754 Par 2262 - Drive it home. Page 657 Par 2264 I am sure now of a re-versal.
Page 878 Par 2633 = shows mind of Judge.
Page 983 Par 2947-48 - there you hit back.
Any one not an idot could see how one sided the whole trial was. The Court of Appeals are not included. Now I am going to sum up. All six of my children 1 grandchild - 1 step child have testified in my behalf. They went thru a lot of misery and what did they accomplish? Absolutely nothing. The D.A. has las word and that - counts. He said - you know blood is thicker than water. There is no

Ask for change of Venue - N.Y. or Queens Co.

grounds for an acquital - except Insanity
now my children cant help me There!
No matter what they might say. It is all
hot air according to the D.A. and the Jury
believe him 9 times out of 10. My only hope
is in the Doctors. So if I get a new trial
dont call any of my children or my g-t.
I shall take the stand in my own behalf.
Now tho not conversant in matters of Law - I
have read of many famous cases - where the charge
was 1st degree Murder. Being a great reader of
the Daily Papers - very little of interest has escaped
me. I always was plain spoken. In reading
over your Summation - I think you not only
wasted your breath - in thanking the Jury
for the attention - they gave you - but your time
as well. It struck me very forcibly that all
the attention the Jury paid - was to the Judge
and The D.a. I saw that - all thru the trial.
Now as an ex - D. a. just refer to your own
exp. You had the last word there and you
got convictions. So then why thank any - one
for something you - did - not - get

#11

grounds for an aqquital - except insanity now my children cant help me there. No matter what they might say it is all hot air according to the D.A. and the jury believe him 9 times out of 10. My only hope is in the Doctors. So if I get a new trial dont call any of my children or my g-d. I shall take the stand in my own behalf.

Now tho not conversant in matters of Law - I have read of many famous cases - where the charge was 1st degree murder. Being a great reader of the Daily Papers - very little of interest has escaped me. I always was - plain spoken. In reading on your summation - I think you not only wasted your breath - in thanking the jury for the attention - they gave you - but your time as well. It struck me very forcibly that all the attention the Jury paid was to the Judge and the D.A. I saw that - all thru the trial. Now as an ex-D.A. just refer to your own exp. You had the last word then and you got convictions. So then why thank any-one for something - you - did - not - get.

stress the fact that when we - 'the girl and I'
reached Worthington. I had entirely forgotten
the key things needed to accomplish the feat
I had in mind. As soon as train stopped
at station I had stepped off and was holding
up my hands for her to jump in my arms.
No thought of the tools. Girl remembers I had
brought a package - sees my empty hands.
Says 'oh' you have forgotten your package. Runs
back to seat where it had been left and gets it.
Had she jumped in his arms when he said
jump - instead of looking for the package - the
waiting conductor would have given the
signal to the engineer. The train would have
gone on carrying the tools - out of his reach.
The child would now - be in her own home
and defendant would not be - where he is.
Had he murder in his heart - would he have got
up from his seat - with package - in front of him.
Took the child by the hand and as soon as train
stopped got off. The child and the tools were paramount
to one another. Without the - tools the child
would have been - useless to him. He could
not have done the deed - it is prescience - he had
in mind. That must is a logical fact -
The main issue - as I see it - in entire - case

stress the fact = that when we - 'the girl and I' reached Washington. I had entirely forgotten the very things needed to accomplish the deed I had in mind. As soon as train stopped at station I had stepped off and was holding up my hands for her to jump in my arms. No thought of the tools. Girl remembers I had brought a package - sees my empty hands. Says 'oh' you have forgotten your package. Runs back to seat where it had been left and gets it. Had she jumped in his arms when he said jump - instead of looking for the package - the waiting conductor - would have given the signal to the Engineer. The train would have gone on carrying the tools - out of his reach. The child would now - be in her own home and defendent would not be - where he is. Had he murder in his heart - would he have got up from his seat - with package - in front of him. Took the child by the hand and as soon as trains stopped got off. The child and the tools are paramount to one another. Without the - tools the child would have been - useless to him. He could not have done the deed - it is presumed - he had in mind. That much is a logical fact - the main issue - as I see it - in entire - case

Some might say - how do we know he forgot all
about the tools. Got off train and the girl ran back
and got them. Take his confession - each of them
described the old house - the stairway the room in
which the act was done. the room in which he
hid - naked - as he called to girl to come up. He
described everything in all its horror. Holding
back nothing. He seemed to glory in the fact he
was weaving a net around himself. He let
the Police to the exact spot - he had described
and they found - the tools - everything - just as
he had placed them. Is that the act of a sane man
here is another point - standing as the girl did at the
top of the steps of the car. It was impossible for
her to see the package - as it stood - one end on the
floor of car - leaning against the side. of the car.
therefore it must have been - his empty hands
she noticed - that caused her to say - oh you have
forgot your package and ran back out got it.
there is no premeditation there. His mind was
pre - occupied - his thoughts were elsewhere.

Some might say - how do we know he forgot all about the tools. Got off train and the girl ran back and got them.. Take his confessions - each of them described the old house - the stairway the room in which the act was done. The room in which he hid - naked - as he called to girl to come up. He described every thing in all its horror. Holding back nothing. He seemed to glory in the fact he was weaving a web around himself. He led the Police to the exact spot - he had descried and they found - the bones - every thing just as he had placed them. Is that an act of a sane man. Here is another point - standing as the girl did at the top of the steps of the car. It was impossible for her to see the package - as it stood - one end on the floor of car - leaning against the side - of the car. Therefore it must have been - his empty hands she noticed - that caused her to say - oh you have forgot your package and run back and get it. There is no premeditation there. His mind was - pre - occupied - his thoughts were elsewhere.

I completed the story of my life – 268 pages it goes into every detail. Covering not only my own life but of my ancestors. Dr Baker has it. After reading it three times – he was so <u>interested</u> he read it <u>over again.</u> <u>He</u> has never expressed to me what he thought of the mental state of the one who wrote it. He may do so to you – if you ask him. I am sure Drs Jelliff & Wertham would be much interested. I did not write it as a mental task tho it may be useful – even there. The object I <u>had in</u> view – was the raising of <u>much needed money.</u> Father McCaffrey says if you see the Warden and tell him <u>you need</u> the story in preparing your <u>case</u> <u>for appeal</u> – he will no doubt turn it over to you. Dr Baker has the record of my case. He is much interested in the medical – testimony. Since I came here he has had many long <u>talks</u> with me. From these and the story of my life – he has read I am sure he can give expert testimony. If I get a new trial – ~~sojourn here~~

I completed the story of my life - 268 Pages it goes into every detail. Covering not only my own life but of my ancestors. Dr Baker has it. After reading it thru once - he was so interested he read it over again. He has never expressed to me - what he thought of the mental state of the one who wrote it. He may do so to you - if you ask him. I am sure Drs Jellip & Wertham would be much interested. I did not write it as a mental task tho it may be useful - even then. The object I had in view - was the raising of much needed money Father McCaffrey says if you see the Warden and tell him you need the story in preparing your case for appeal - he will no doubt turn it over to you. Dr Baker has the record of my case. He is much interested in the Medical testimony. Since I am here he has had many long talks with me. From them and the story of my life - he has read I am sure he can give expert testimony. If I get a new trial - sobpoena him.

#12.

Father Mc Caffery spoke of some one here
who was convicted of 1st deg murder and
granted a new trial. His counsel asked
for a change of Venue — it was granted
and he won out. The whole record of my
trial proves its un-fairness to me. I am
sure you have good grounds on which to
ask for a change of Venue. Try it out
I spent 46 months in 5 Sanitariums and was
confined for mental observation in two Hospitals
in N.Y. City. Hence the fact that what I saw—
men put in straight jackets and strapped down
to beds. The screams and yells I heard did not
improve a some what shaky mental condition
Rev A. W. Peterson would like you to call
at his office before you go

#12

Father Mc Caffery spoke of some one here who was convicted of 1st deg murder and granted a new trial. His counsel asked for a change of venue - it was granted and he won out. The whole record of my trial proves its un-fairness to me. I am sure you have good grounds on which to ask for a change of venue. Try it out I spent 46 months in 5 Sanitariums and was confined for mental observation in two Hospitals in N.Y. City. Stress the fact that what I saw - men put in straight jackets and strapped down to beds. The screams and yells I head did not impress a some what shaky mental condition Rev A. W. Peterson would like you to call at his office before you go

  Sheriff   EAST VIEW, NEW YORK.   Warden

Fiel.

To.   _Phytophiler._   Tier No.   Cell No.

Street & No.   [1935?]

City   State   Date II-24-35 193 .

Speaking of Flowers

In the section of Washington D.C. where I lived when a boy. We had a large park with flowers of all kind. I always loved to see and smell them. Those I loved best were Roses — Holly hoks — Lilacs — Sweet Peas — Honeysuckle. I often saw pictures in windows of male and female figures in a Nude state. Garlands of vines and flowers, draped about their "nakedness." I always had a strong desire to appear in Public absolutely naked, or decked out in flowers. I of course realized I could not appear in the streets in such a garb. However I did so in my room at night. I would buy a few leaves or vines now and then a rose or lilac. Strip naked and array myself in every possible way. stick stems of roses up my penis & behind. Then I would take a small looking glass in my hand. Tilt mirror of dresser on a slant and view my naked body for hours.* Then eat the petals of roses. Then this became interested in Nudist Colonies and wrote to Naual

* Then I eat one. Shortly after sticking in flowers. Mostly in front — sleep in peace.

VISITING DAYS— WEDNESDAY and SATURDAY— 1:30 P.M. to 3 P.M.
VISITING DAYS—WEDNESDAY AND SATURDAY FROM 1:30 P.M. to 3 P.M.

(Hurt?)* Yes, at first. But I seemed to — to want it.

Phytophilia

Speaking of Flowers

In the section of Washington D.C. where I lived when a boy. We had a large yard with flowers of all kinds. I always loved to see and smell them. Those I loved best were Roses - Holly hoks - Lilacs - Sweet Peas - Honeysuckle. I often saw pictures in windows of male and female figures in a nude state. Garlands of vines and flowers, draped about their (nakedness). I always had a strong desire to appear in Public absolutely naked, or decked out in flowers. I of course realized I could not appear in the streets in such a garb. However I did so in my room at night. I would buy a few leaves or vines now and then a rose or lilac. Strip Naked and annoy myself in every possible way stick stems of roses up my penis & behind. Then I would take a small looking glass in my hand. Tilt mirror of dresser on a slant and view my naked body for hours.* Then eat the petals of roses. Thru this became interested in Nudist Colonies and wrote to same.

*then I wd come. Shortly after sticking in flowers. Mostly in front - stem in penis. (Hurt?) 'Yes at first. But I seemed to - to want it.'

Phyto-philia

Very fond of flowers. Like to see them and to smell them. Sometimes I have them roses, with a stem of about 3 inches, lilacs & other flowers struck the stem in penis it hurts but I seemed to put a prick out of it, a thrill, I stuck them up my behind to [ease] my. Many times I came when the rose & other flowers was in my penis. I was crazy, naked when I done it. Also came when wearing it in his behind. I have a gilded glass in my dresser, so that I can see myself. Sometimes I hold a little mirror & look at myself. I stood sometimes for an hour holding the little mirror in my hand, so that I can get a view of my back with the rose in it. Bright beautiful roses. I then when the rose out & ate the petals. I often take string of green twigs like vine or honeysuckle & bound them around my prick & my behind both in the glass at myself; often came like that. Always got a hard one.

For a while worked in a flower store in Washington, Cora Strauss one of the biggest flower stores in Washington. That's where I got absorbed.

Phyto-philia

Very fond of flowers. Like to see them - like to smell them. Sometimes I have - when roses with a stem of about 3 inches, lilacs & other flowers, stuck the stem in penis, it hurts but I seemed to get a rush out of it, a thrill, I stuck them up my behind to same my. Many times I came when the rose. ones after flower was in my penis. I was a boy when I done that. Alvin came when having it in his behind. I have a looking glass in my drawer, so that I can see myself. Sometimes I hold a little mirror to look at myself. I stood emotions for an hour, holding the little mirror in my hand, so that I can get a mirror of my inch with the rose in it. Bought beautiful roses. I then when to ease rose out & ate the petals. I often pushed string of green try I like vines or honeysuckle, & bound them around my body my pricks or my behind, back in the, can at any self, after came like that. Alonzo got a hairy one.

For a while worked in a flower store in Washington, Cora Strauss, on of the biggest flower stores in Washington. HUTLY, where I was unobserved.

354 Hunter Street

Ossining, N. Y.

Dec 1 _____ 1935

Your Excellency

I was born at Washington D.C. May 19-1870.
Of a well known and respectable family. The name
of Fisk has long been an honored one - in all walks
of life. I am the first one - to bring disgrace upon it.
My father Capt Randall Fisk was well known. He
dropped dead in the street Oct 16-1875. Thru the Masonic
fraternity - he was a 32 d Mason. My mother was placed
in the U. S. Treasury in 1876. She remained there
septs 1885. At the age of 5 I was placed by my mother
in St Johns Orphanage - remaining there two years.
During that time I learned to lie - beg and steal.
Saw both boys and girls - older than I - do all kinds
of immoral acts. I had a brother Walter H. Fisk
who served 5 yrs in the U. S. Navy. He had been all
over the World. The tales he told on his visits home -
of savages - cannibals - torture - were to me marvelous.
At that time what he said impressed me greatly.
When I left the Home - I was sent to Sunday School
and was a choir boy in St Johns P. E. Church 1880 - 4
Dr Robert Reyburn - one of the doctors who attended
President James A. Garfield. when he was shot
in 1881. Was my Sunday School Supt. In 1894 I came
to N.Y. City. My first job was at Sanford Hall —
Flushing N.Y. It was a private Sanitarium — run

108

Gov Herbert H. Lehman
State House
Albany N.Y.

Your Excellency

I was born at Washington D.C. May 19- 1870 - of a well known and respectable family. The name of Fish - has long been an honored one in all walks of life. I am the first one - to bring disgrace upon it. My father Capt Randall Fish - was well known. He dropped dead in the street Oct 16 - 1875. Thru the Masonic fraternity - he was a 32d Mason. My mother was placed in the U.S. Treasury in 1876. She remained there upto 1885. At the age of 5 I was placed by my mother in St Johns Orphanage - remaining there two years. During that time I learned - to lie- beg - and steal. Saw both boys and girls - older than I - do all kinds on immoral acts. I had a brother Walter H. Fish who served 5 yrs in the U.S. Navy. He had been all over the world. The tales he told on his visits home - of savages - cannibals - torture - were to me marvelous. At that time what he said impressed me greatly. When I left the Home - I was sent to Sunday School and was a choir boy in the St Johns P.E. Church 1880-4 Dr. Robert Reyburn - one of the doctors who attended President James A. Garfield when he was shot in 1881. Was my Sunday School Supt. In 1894 I came to N.Y. City. My first job was at Sanford Hall -- Flushing N.Y. It was a private sanitarium run

354 Hunter Street

Ossining, N. Y.

193

#2

by Dr. Richard L. Browne. He had an overige of about 200 Patients. I was there 26 months April 1894 June 1896. I have done work in four other places of the same kind. In 1929 I was with Dr. Robert B. Lamb Harmon N.Y. I am a Painter by trade — all my life I have worked in homes both Public & private. My greatest delight was children — I have six '6' of my own. Five '5' grand children — eight '8' step-children. Not to speak of those I met in private homes. I was Sexton of St Ann's P. E. Church — 140 St & Ann's Av. 1920-1. I was Sexton of Bethany M. E. Church 67 st & 1 st Av. 1923-4. Janitor of a School at Flushing N.Y. Jane — work at Mary Lium Home for convalescent children — at White Plains N.Y. and at Barnabus Home 304 Mul Ferry St. of which Bishop Wm T. Manning is president. Then can any one say — I ever harmed the hair of the head — of any child. While I was arrested Police and others tried to make me confess to many other crimes. If I came to face my Maker — today I can say — that in confessing this one — I have cleared my soul. I lay the beginning — of all my trouble — to my wife. We were all living happily together at College Point N.Y. I was away from home a good deal she took in a boarder. John Strouble by name. Jan 19-1917 my wife sent '5' of the children — to the movies. She

by Dr Richard L. Browne. He had an average of about 200 Patients. I was there 26 months April 1874 June 1896. I have done work in four other places of the same kind. IN 1929 I was with Dr Robert B. Lamb Harmon N.Y. I am a Painter by trade - all my life I have worked in homes both Public & private. My greatest delight was children - I have six '6' of my own. Five '5' grand children - eight '8' step-children. Not to speak of those I met in prvte homes. I was Sexton of St Anns P.E. Church - 140th st St Anns on 1920-1. I was Sexton of Bethany M.E. Church 69 st & 1st on 1923-4. Janitor of a school at Flushing N.Y. Done work at Mary Linn Home for Convalescent children - at White Plains N.Y. and at Barnabas Home 304 Mulberry st - of which Bishop Wm F. Manning is president. Never can any one say - I ever harmed the hair of the head - of any child. When I was arrested Police and others tried to make me confess to many other crimes. If I was to face my Maker - today I can say - that in confessing this one - I have cleared my soul. I lay the beginning - of all my trouble - to my wife. We were all living happily together at College Point N.Y. I was away from home a good deal she took in a boarder - John Stroube by name. Jan 19- 1917 my wife sent '5' of the children - to the movies. The

#3

show was food and like all children - They stayed as long as possible. Especially on a cold winters night - when they got back home - to find a nice warm home and a good hot supper awaiting them. Instead of that this is what they found - Their mother gone and the house empty. While they were at the show - she stripped the house bare. Unknown to the children she had made arrangements- to sell everything in the house and go off with the boarder. Not so much as a blanket to wrap about our youngest child - then 3 yrs & 4 mo of age - did she leave. Now Your Excellency - you are a husband and a father can you imagine - what my poor children thought. Place any man you know of - in the same position and once more imagine what a shock - he would get to receive such a telegram - as I received from my daughter then 16. Papa come home - Mama gone - house empty. I came at once of course and had to rent a furnished apartment until we had found a new home and trying - all over again. The names and ages of my six '6' children - at that time was as follows. Albert H. Jr 18- Anna 16- Gertrude -13- Eugene 10- John 7- Henry 3-4 mo I was advised to put the 3 youngest- in a home. But I had enough of homes - when quite a boy.

112

#3

show was good and like all children - they stayed as long as possible. Expecting on a cold winters night - when they got back home - to find a nice warm home and a good hot supper waiting there. Instead of that this is what they found - their mother gone and the house empty. While they were at the show - she stripped the house bare. Unknown to the children she had made arrangements - to sell everything in the house and go off with the boarder. Not so much as a blanket - to wrap about our youngest child - then 3 yrs & 4 mo of age - did she leave. Now Your Excellency - you are a husband and a father can you imagine - what my four children thought. Place any man you know of - in the same position - and once more imagine what a shock he would get - to receive such a telegram - as I received from my daughter then 16. Papa come home - Mama gone - house empty. I came at once of course and had to rent a furnished apartment until we had found a new home and begin - all oer again. The names and ages of my six '6' children - at that time was as follows. Albert H. Jr 18 - Anna 16 - Gertrude - 13 - Eugene 10 - John 7 - Henry 3-4 mo. I was advised to put the 3 youngest - in a home. But I had enough of homes - when quite a boy.

4

I stuck to them — as they can all tell you. Was mother
as well as father — until they were old enough to
to to work or marry. Their mother — "still living" is
in the eyes of the law — my wife. I never divorced
her. She is still living with this same man and
has 3 children by him. I have never really been
the same man since that night. While I am now
as sane as I ever was. My past life is proof positive
that on June 3 — 1928 — I could not possibly have been
in my right mind. Had I been the child would
now — be in her home and I would never of had
to write this letter — to you. I did not receive a fair
and impartial trial. If you will read over the
brief of Mr James Dempsey. Your own eyes will
answer you of that fact. I most humbly ask
Your Excellency — to spare my life

I am very truly

Albert H. Fish 90272

P. S.

In that brief you will find opinions of two
members of the Court Of Appeals — Hon justices
Cardoza and Lehman

#4

I stuck to them - as they can all tell you. Was Mother as well as father - until they were old enough to go to work or marry. Their mother - 'still living' is in the eyes of the law - my wife. I never divorced her. She is still living with this same man and has 3 children by him. I have never really been the same man since that night. While I am now as sane as I ever was. My past life is proof positive that on June 3 - 1928 - I could not possibly have been - in my right mind. Had I been the child would now - be in her home and I would never of had to write this letter - to you. I did not receive a fair and impartial trial. If you will read on the brief of Mr James Dempsey. Your own eyes will assure you of that fact. I most humbly ask Your Excellency - to spare my life.

I am very truly
Albert H. Fish 90272

P.S.

     In that brief you will find opinions of two members of the Court of Appeals - Hon Justices Cardoza and Lehman.

Budd Skeleton To Hold Fish As Murderer

The disjointed bones retrieved from the Westchester woodlot where Grace Budd was murdered

Albert H. Fish

were reconstructed into a skeleton yesterday and positively identified by Dr. Amos O. Squire, County Medical Examiner, as those of a child less than 12.

Columbia University anatomists, using seventy to eighty fragments, rebuilt the skeleton and thus provided authorities with a corpus delicti on which to base a charge of first degree murder against Albert H. Fish, the wizened sadist who admitted the slaying.

Thomas F.Reynolds,   WESTCHESTER COUNTY JAIL,   George A. Casey,
        Sheriff   EAST VIEW, NEW YORK.   Warden

To.   Tier No.   Cell No.

Street & No.   Dont forget   Dale 19 - 1917
City   State   Date   193 .

Pa or Va man lured widow and 4 boys
to prison cellar of his home. Tortured
and killed all five for insurance. Bodies
found cut in many pieces   cells.

Hanneman Butcher of Germany 1914
War- meat scarce and very high. Lured
34 young men & boys- who were well built.
Cut them up and sold their flesh in his
butcher shop. When arrested there was a photo
and history of above in my scrip See M. F. W. King.

I always had a desire to roast meat cut
from a boy and eat it. That Sunday before
I put on my clothes. I cut off her breasts-
some of her belly- legs and all the meat
I could get off her behind. I took it home
and broiled it on gas. Taste like Veal

dont forget Vision mist Chink Sunday
  "   "   "   " guard Pat Fitzgerald
about 2 All He can tell you

VISITING DAYS- WEDNESDAY and SATURDAY- 1:30 P.M. to 3 P.M.
VISITING DAYS- WEDNESDAY AND SATURDAY FROM 1:30 P.M. to 3 P.M.

Dont forget Jan 19- 1917

Pa or Va man lured widow and 4 boys to prison cellar of his home. Tortured and killed all five for insurances. Bodies found cut in many pieces   cells.

Haarmann Butcher of Germany 1914 War - meat scarce and very high. Lured 24 young men & boys - who were well built. Cut them up and sold their flesh in his butcher shop. When arrested there was a photo and history of over in my grip see Wm F.W. King.

I always had a desire to roast meat cut from a boy and eat it. That Sunday before I put on my clothes. I cut off her breasts - some of her belly - legs and all the meat I could get off the behind. I took it home and broiled it on our gas. Taste like veal.

Dont forget Vision with chink Sunday
"   "   "   "   guard Pat Fitzgerald
about 2 Am He can tell you

(unnumbered)

Edward Hickman California
District court dead girl - Cut up her body

Holmes & Sharwood - Stripped naked
beaten and hung to trees in the presence of
15,000 men & women boys & girls - California

Guiseppe - Mrs Mack - Sharme
Body cut in 14 pieces - found in river -

Many Negroes stripped - mutilated & burned

Bobby Franks Chicago

Charles Northrop California - Had a farm
Lured small boys as berry pickers stripped
them naked - tied them up in hay loft and
whipped and tortured them to death. Cut off
bodies, parts of flesh missing 4 or 5 boys. Two
brothers 10-12. His Mother involved bodies found

Admiral Perry Expedition & N.P.
Some of crew eaten, to keep others alive

120

Cases I took an interest In
                        (animated)

Edward Hickman California
Dismebemded girl - cut up her body

Holmes & Thornwood - stripped naked beaten and hung to trees in the presence of
15,000 men & women boys & girls - California

Guldunseppe - Mrs Mack - Thorne
Body cut in 14 pieces - found in river -

Many negroes stripped - mutilated & burned

Bobby Franks Chicago

Charles Northrop California - Had a farm Lured small boys as berry pickers stripped
them naked - tied them up in hog loft and whipped and tortured them to death. Cut up
bodies, parts of flesh missing 4 or 5 boys. Two brothers 10-12. His mother involved,
bodies found

Admiral Perry Exposition to N.P. three of crew eaten to keep others alive

Had a Sunstroke when 17 or in 1887
in Washin D.C. Many queer things since.
Feb 5-1898 Married 1st wife, 6 children
all living. She was 19 - I 28 - 37 yrs married
—— 1930 Married 2nd wife she had boy
& twin, none by me. Left her at 4011 Hill ave
Feb 5 1930 Married 3rd wife at Columbus Ohio
she had 7 children none by me
—— 1930 Married 4th wife Waterloo Iowa
she had 3 children none by me
I never obtained a divorce from any

Married all of them under own name.
Unnatural relations with them all

In order to prove to you that I am
not faking and also to back up your
own convictions, borrow a tin cup
from pantry and I will drink my
own urine, eat my own # 2

           (Over)

122

Fish

Marriages

Had a sunstroke when 17 or in 1887 in Washin D.C. Many queer things since. Feb 5-
1898 Married 1st wife, 6 children all living. She was 19 - I 28-37 yrs married
-- 1930 Married 2nd wife she had boy of ten, none by me. Left her at 4011 Hill Ave
Feb 5 1930 Married 3rd wife at Columbus Ohio she had 7 children none by me
-- 1930 Married 4th wife Waterloo Tower She had 3 children none by me
I never obtained a divorce from any

Married all of them under own name.
Unatural relations with them all

In order to prove to you that I am not faking and also to back your own convictions,
borrow a tin cup from pantry and I will drink my own urine, eat my own #2

     (over)

gloomy spells.
I had frequent gloomy spells and imagined my own children did not want me in their homes. None of them did anything to give me that impression. On such occasions I left their homes and rented a furnished room. Then you see while with them I could not indulge in the practices it was impossible for me to resist

gloomy spells

I had frequent gloomy spells and imagined my own children, did not want me in their homes. None of them did anything to give me that impression. On such occasions I left their homes and rented a furnished room. Then you see while with them I could not indulge in the practices it was impossible for me to resist

BUDD MURDER SITE YIELDS MORE BONES

30 Are Dug From Under House, Causing Fear That Others May Have Been Slain There.

DARIEN CRIME LINK SOUGHT

Suspect Admits He Was There in March—Child's Skeleton Found 3 Months Later.

God said suffer little children to
come into Me and forbid them not - for
of such is the kingdome of Heaven

I saved that child from a fate far wase
than death, when I slew her

O ye daughter of Babylon: Blessed is
he that rewardeth them as thou servest us.

Hoppy is he that takath thy little ones
and dasheth their head against the stonds.
        Psalm 137- 8- 9- tene

Blessed is the man who correcteth
his son in whom he delictith with
stripes for great shall be his reward.

128

Halluc. + delus.

God said suffer little children to come into me and forbid them not - for of such is the kingdom of Heaven

I saved that child from a fate far worse than death, when I seen her

O ye daughter of Babylon: Blessed is he that servasdeth them as thou servest us.

Happy is he that taketh thy little ones and dasheth their head against the stones. Psalms 137 - 8-9 - Verse

Blessed is the man who correctith his son in whom he delictith with stripes for great shall be his reward.

As he was about to plunge the knife
into his body. His hand was stayed
by an Angel of the Lord.

I have sinned grievously and they are
ever before me. My only hope for the life
to come. Is thru the rod. Should I
be found of a feeble mind and sent to a
Hospital. I ask you Sir and your fellow
workers in my behalf, In Gods Name
recommend to the Dr in charge that I
be soundly whipped at least twice daily
as long as I am there. No greater favor
can I ask of any man

Blessed is the man, who loveth his son
and spareth not the rod

It is better to receive Stripes, than to
go down into hell

            (Book of Proverbs)

God has ordained that I Revenge myself on Sin

130

As he was about to plunge the knife into his body. His hand was stayed by an Angel of the Lord.

I have sinned griveously and they are ever before me. My only hope for the life to come. Is thru the rod. Should I be found of a feeble mind and sent to a Hospital. I ask you Dr and your fellow workers in my behalf, In Gods Name reccommend to the Dr in charge that I be soundly whipped at least twice daily as long as I am there. No greater favor I can ask of any man.

Blessed is the man, who loveth his son and spareth not the rod

It is better to receive Stripes, than to go down into hell.

(Book of Proverbs)

God has ordained that I Purge myself on sin thru the rod

Episode with 19 yo. old boy Thomas.   Thomas Kedden

Keep him 10 days in room before finding I can not house; 5 wks. then before leaving him. That was about 19th. That sadistic overwhelming. Intended to use him first, then torture him to death, then use the parts that appealed to me for food. I craved to hear someone scream & yelling.

About 25 yrs ago, or when I was 40 - I was doing a painting job in Wilmington Del. I was rooming near job on outskirts of city. Met a well built boy of 19. He had ran away from home in Arkansas on acct of being stripped naked and whipped by a brutal step dad. He had a pretty face, would pass for 16 except for his size. Looked like a girl. He appeared to be kind & silly. He told me his story. Some one back home, told him he could get a job in Du Ponts. He beat his way in empty R.R. cars and by foot. When he got to Wilmington he was told no more help were needed. He was silly in his actions and map. Tho going on 20 and as strong as an ox. He was as easy to spank & switch as a boy of ten. He rode for two days in a banana car. Floor was covered with straw. Five men regular hoboes used him dog and night. His behind was so sore from them, it hurt him when he walked. He said all of them made him suck them off. At first he spit it out, but they beat him on his bare behind with their belts and made him swallow it. He had the prettiest and fattest behind I ever saw on a man. But he was covered from his neck down to his shins, with long black hair. You could hardly see his dickey or behind from hair.

#1
Episode with 19 yr. old boy Thomas

Thomas Kedden

Kept him 10 days in room before finding the old house; 5 wks. there before leaving him. That was about 1910. First sadistic overwhelming. Intended to use him first, then torture him to death, then use the parts that appealed to me for food - I craved to hear someone scream & yell.

About 25 years ago, or when I was 40 - I was doing a Painting job in Wilmington Del. I was rooming near Job on outskirts of city. Met a well built boy of 19. He had ran away from home in Arkansas on acct of being stripped naked and whipped by a brutal step Dad. He had a pretty face, would pass for 16 except for his size. Looked like a girl. He appeared to be kind of silly. He told me his story. Some one back home, told him he could get a job in Du Ponts. He beat his way in empty R.R. cars and by foot. When he got to Wilmington he was told no moore help were needed. He was silly in his actions and ways. Tho going on 20 and as strong as an ox. He was as easy to spank & switch as a boy of ten. He rode for two days in a banana car. Floor was covered with straw. Five men regular hoboes used him day and night. His behind was so sore from them it hurt him when he walked. He said all of them made him suck them off. At first he spit it out, but they beat him on his bare behind, with their belts and made him swallow it. He had the prettiest ad fattest behind I eve saw on a man. But he was covered from his neck down to his shins, with long black hair. You could hardly see his dickey or behind from hair.

#2 When I first met him he had not a cent and was almost starved, no place to lay his head. I took him with me, to the place where I got my meals and we had supper. How he did eat, I enjoyed watching him and filled him up. Then I took him to my room for just what I wanted. I knew he was Lousey for he could not stop scratching. I made him take everything off. He was full of the biggest lice I ever saw. His clothes were full, his shoes and hat worn out, I threw them out. I let good warm water run in the bath tub, until it was half full. Then I made him get in and sit flat on his behind. I told him to stay there until I got back. I went to a drug store and got a package of hair remover. in a powdered form I had a pair of clippers and I cut all the long hair off him. Then I got a tin can dumped the powder in it and added water. This made a Paste. I smeared it all over him. Let it stand ten minuets. Then I made him sit down in tub and took a Sponge and a cake of soap. I washed him good, Then made him stand up, When I touched his back, belly, behind and Dick, every hair fell off. Then he was really naked and how pretty he looked. A nice big dickey and a fat behind. I wiped him dry. Then rubbed him all over with hair tonic. I loved him then and kissed him all over

#2

When I first met him he had not a cent and was almost stoned, no place to lay his head. I took him with me, to the place where I got my meals and we had supper. How he did eat. I enjoyed watching him and filled him up. Then I took him to my room for just what I wanted. I knew he was Lousey for he could not stop scratching. I made him take everything off. He was full of the biggest lice I ever seen. His clothes were full, his shoes, and hat worn out, I threw them out. I let good warm water run in the bath tub, until it was half full. Then I made him get in and sit flat on his behind. I told him to stay there until I got back. I went to a drug store and got a package of hair remover in a powdered form. I had a pair of clippers and I cut all the long hair off him. Then I got a tin can dumped the powder in it and added water. This made a Paste. I smeared it all on him. Let it stand ten minuets. Then I made him sit down in tub and took a spongue and a cake of soap. I washed him good, then made him stand up. When I touched his back - belly - behind and Dick, every hair fell off. Then he was really naked and how pretty he looked. A nice big dickey and fat behind. I wiped him dry. Then rubbed him all over with hair tonic. I loved him then and kissed him all over

#3 Then the fun began. It was a warm
night and I went out and got a qt of ice cream.
We eat about half of it. Then I stripped naked
and got in bed. He kissed me in the mouth
many times, my breast - belly - legs - dicky behind.
I put ice cream in his behind and all on his
dicky then licked it off. He done the same with me.
Then I made him lay on my knees, face down
a I sat on side of bed. How sweet and pretty
his bare naked ass looked to me. I kissed it a
100 times square in his sweet honey pot. Then I
tok my hair brush and used the back of it to
spank him. I made him yell Ouch papa I will
be a good boy. Yes I spanked him on his nice fat
ass until it looked like a ripe tomato all over.
Then it was his turn to be Papa. I was his boy
and had done #2 in my pants. He gave me a bath
then sat on side of bed and made me lay across
his knees face down. He spanked my bare ass good
and plenty. Made me yell - Ouch papa I wont
do #2 in my pants again. I spanked him till
he cried - he made me cry too. My ass was all red
when he got thru. I saw it in the looking glass.
How good it felt, when he spanked, but it hurt
and I always wanted more and give him more.
Nearly all night, we had fun. I sucked him off
first; then he sucked me off. We played with
each other and rested. Then I took vaseline

#3

Then the fun began. It was a warm night and I went out and got a qt of ice cream. We eat about half of it. Then I stripped naked and got in bed. He kissed me in the mouth many times, my breast - belly - legs - dicky behind. I put ice cream in his behind and all on his dickey then licked it off. He done the same with me. Then I made him lay down on his knees, face down as I sat on side of bed. How sweet and pretty his bare naked ass looked to me. I kissed it a 100 times square in his sweet honey pot. Then I took my hair brush and used the back of it - to spank him. I made him yell ouch papa I will be a good boy. Yes I spanked him on his nice fat ass untied it, looked like a ripe tomato all over. Then it was his turn to be Papa. I was his boy and had done #2 in my pants. He gave me a bath then sat on side of bed and made me lay across his knees face down. He spanked my bare ass good and plenty. Made me yell - Ouch papa I wont do #2 in my pants again. I spanked him till he cried - he made me cry too. My ass was all red when he got thru. I saw it in the looking glass. How good it felt, when he spanked, but it hurt and I always wanted more and give him more. Nearly all night, we had fun. I sucked him off first, then he sucked me off. We played with each other and rested. Then I took Vasoline

#4) and pried and some ice his behind
Also in my own. Then I stuck my dickey
up his behind. He had a large syrup bowl and
it went all the way up. How good it felt as I
shoved it in. It slipped out once or twice. Then
he did it to me. We put our arms around each
other, kissed and went to sleep. I bought him
some clothes. That went on for about ten days.
Now I had whipped many boys and girls but
they were gagged so they could make no out cry.
I craved for something different. I wanted
to lash - cut - burn a nice big fat pretty bare
ass like Thomas had. Torture him, hear him
scream with pain. I could not do it here -
to many people. I began to look around. About
a mile away there was an old farm house.
It had the name of being haunted. No one had
lived in it for several yrs. It stood back
from the road about 200 ft, back of it was the
barn. Three stalls and room for a carriage.
Upstairs hay loft and coachmans room. In
it was a bed and a chair. The door and lock was
in good order with a key. It was just the place
to whip and torture Thomas just as I wished.
I put a chamber in the room for him & use.
Then one rainy day I bought a blanket and
we came to the torture chamber. I made him
strip bare naked and locked him in. Then

and smeared some in his behind also in my own. Then I stuck my dickey up his behind. He had a large sugar bowl and it went all the way up. How good it felt as I shoved it in. It slipped out once or twice. Then he did it to me. We put our arms around each other kissed and went to sleep. I bought him some clothes. That went on for about ten days. How I had whipped many boys and girls but they were gagged so they could make no out no cry. I craved for something different. I wanted to Lash - cut - burn a nice big fat pretty bare ass like Thomas had. Torture him, hear him scream with pain. I could not do it here- to many people. I began to look around. About a mile away there was an old farm house. It had the name of being haunted. No one had lived it in for several yrs. It stood back form the road about 200 ft, back of it was the barn. Three stalls and room for a carriage. Upstairs hog loft and Coachmans room. In it was a bed and a chair. The door and lock was in good order with a key. It as just the place to whip and torture Thomas just as I wished. I put a chamber in the room for him to use. Then one rainy day I bought a blanket and we came to the torture chamber. I made him strip bare naked and locked him in. Then

#5) I went back to my room. Next day... I did not go to work... I bought a sharp knife, box of matches and a Pt of alcohol. I went back to the old house and got his clothes and put them with the other things in one of the stalls. There was a well in the yard, nice cold water. I filled an old pitcher full of water and gave it to him to drink. Then I cut about 20 switches off black berry bushes. They were full of thorns. I brought 2 book straps they use in school. I took my 3 switches and the straps and tied his hands behind him, then his feet. Now I said to him I have you, just where I want you and the way I intend to keep you for next 2 weeks. Then I turned him over on his belly and began to torture his nice fat ass. I used one switch at a time. Struck him as hard as I could. Each blow the thorns stuck in his flesh. Often I would drag the switch instead of lifting it. Then it would tare out rip the cheeks of his fat ass. How he did scream. It was sweet music to my very soul to hear him and know that no one else could. Then I spanked him. How the blood did spatter on the blanket and all over the wall. Then I took the knife and slit his fat ass between the cheeks. I held my mouth to his ass and sucked the blood. Then I filled the pitcher with water untied his hands, locked him in and went home. Next evening I brought out the blanket a small hammer - tacks - 6 candles. Then I

#5

I went back to my room. Next day I did not go to work.. I bought a sharp knife, box of matched and a pt of alcohol. I went back to the old house and got his clothes and put them with the other things in one of the stalls. There was a well in the yard, nice cold water. I filled an old pitcher full of water and gave it to him to drink. Then I cut about 20 switches off black berry bushes. They were full of thorns. I brought 2 book straps they use in school. I took up 3 switches and the straps and tied his hand behind him, then his feet. Now I said to him, I have you, just where I want you and the way I intend to keep you for next 2 weeks. Then I turned him over on his belly and began to torture his nice fat ass. I used one switch at a time. Struck him as hard as I could. Each blow the thorns stuck in his flesh. Often I would drag the switch instead of lifting it. Then It would tare and rip the cheeks of his fat ass. How he did scream. It was sweet music to my very soul to hear him and know that no one else could. Then I spanked him. How the blood did spatter on the blanket and all over the wall. Then I took the knife and slit his fat ass between the cheeks. I held my mouth to his ass and sucked the blood. Then I filled the pitcher with water untied his hands, locked him in and went home. Next evening I brought another blanket a small hammer - tacks - 6 candles. Then I

#6 could work in the day and torture him at night. I tacked blankets our window out by the light of a candle I could see him. For 5 days all he had was water and whippings. Then I bought him sandwiches and coffee. He was so hungry I made him eat his own #2 before I gave him food. Then I made him lay on his back in bed. I turned both of his legs backward over his head and strapped his feet to head of iron bed. Then I had his nice pretty fat ass, turned up to me, to do just whatever I could think of and that was plenty. I jabbed one whole package of needles in the checks of his ass. It looked like a pin cushion. I stuck a pin all the way thru his dickey and one between his 2 balls. That was a Sat night. I left him just as he was and went home. Sunday I bought some food and a bottle of Peroxide. I pulled the needles out of his ass dicky and balls. How the blood did flow where I pulled them out of his dicky. It was as blue as ink. I poured Peroxide on his ass and dick then smeared him good with Vaseline. Then I undid his feet and let him rest, he went to sleep. Then I jabbed a long needle in his belly and he woke up. Then I fed him. From 9 a.m. Sunday until 11 p.m. I whipped - cut and burned his bare ass except at noon and 6 p.m. when I went out for food. To weaken him and keep him so I gave him food but such a dog. I gave him a table spoon and he eat most of his #2 out of the chamber

#6

could work in the day and torture him at night. I tucked blanket over window and by the light of a candle I could see him. For 5 days all he had was water and whippings. Then I brought him sandwiches and coffee. He was so hungry I made him eat his own #2, before I gave him food. Then I made him lay on his back in bed. I turned both of his legs backward on his head and strapped his feet to head of iron bed. Then I had his nice pretty fat ass, turned up to me, to do just what ever I could think of and that was plenty. The whole package of needles in the cheeks of his ass. It looked like a pin cushion. I stuck a pin all the way thru his dickey and one between his 2 balls. That was a Sat. night I left him just as he was all night and went home. Sunday I brought some food and a bottle of Peroxide. I pulled the needles out of his ass dickey and balls. How the blood did pour when I pulled them out of his dickey. It was as blue as ink. I pored Peroxide on his ass and dick then smeared him good with Vasoline. Then I untied his feet and let him rest, he went to sleep, then I jabbed a long needle in his belly and he woke up. Then I fed him. From 9 am Sunday until 11 p.m. I whipped - cut and burned his bare ass except at noon and 6 pm when I went out for food. To weaken him and keep him so I gave him food but once a day, I gave him a table spoon and he eat much of his own #2 out of the chamber

#7/ In a short time, both of us got to like it we called it peanut butter and #1 either. I let him rest about an hour. Then I bent his legs on his head again and tied his feet. I switched him hard between the cheeks of his fat ass and where the thorns stuck in his flesh, I dragged them so they would tare his ass. How he screamed. Then I spilled alcohol on his bare ass and dicky, then set him on fire. I clapped my hands and jumped with joy when I heard him scream. It hurt like hell while it lasted but the alcohol burned off quick. I spanked him and switched his bare ass until I was all tired out. I spread paper on the floor and made him lay on his belly. I stripped naked and done a heap of #2 on his ass. Then I turned him over on his back so he would be full of it. I had some in my behind and sat down on his face and made him lick my bare ass clean with his tongue. But when I knew I had him so weak I could master him. Then I let him play Papa. Everything I done to him I made him do to me. He spanked - switched out and burned my bare ass. He made me jump and yell, when he sunk the thorns in me and then pulled them thru my feet. How I screamed when he set my ass on fire. It hurt but I got a big kick a thrill out of it. Many times when I had him, tied up, I was tempted to slice real cutlets off his nice fat ass. Take them out in the yard. Make a fire and roast

146

#7

In a short time, both of us got to like it we called it peanut butter and #1 cider. I let him rest about an hour. Then I bent his legs over his head again and tied his feet. I switched him hard between the cheeks of his fat ass and when the thorns stuck in his flesh, I dragged them so they would tare his ass. How he screamed. Then I spilled alcohol on his bare ass and dickey, then set him on fire. I clapped my hands and jumped with joy when I heard him scream. It hurt like hell while it lasted but the Alcohol burned off quick. I spanked him and switched his bare ass until I was all tired out. I spread paper on the floor and made him lay on his belly. I stripped naked and done a heap of #2 on his ass. Then I turned him on his back so he would be full of it. I had some in my behind and I sat down on his face and made him lick my bare ass clean with his tongue. But when I knew I had him so weak I could master him. Then I let him play Papa. Everything I done to him I made him do to me. He spanked - switched cut and burned my bare ass. He made me jump and yell, when he sunk the thorns in me and then pulled them thru my flash. How I screamed when he set my ass on fire It hurt but I got a big kick, a thrill out of it. Many times when I had him, tied up, I was temped to slice veal cutlets off his nice fat ass. Take them out in the yard. Make a fire and roast them. My mouth fairly watering to see what it would <u>taste like.</u> I always wanted to eat a <s>big</s> nice fat ass. I also had a strong desire to eat off his prick and balls. Split them open, <s>roast</s> them and eat them. But I knew if I did that I would not have him to torture or be tortured by him. I pissed and shit all on him in his mouth - eyes - Ears. He did to me. I know we eat on 10 lbs of peanut butter and drank several gallons of cider, between us in the 5 weeks I had him. All things have an end. My job was finished and I could not afford to keep him. Realizing that I must go home. I got <u>up</u>, brought him his clothes. He did not want to put them on, but opened my pants, took out my dick and sucked me off. Then I was tempted I tied him up again, played with his dickey until it got stiff. Then I took the knife and sliced off <u>half of it.</u> I shall never forget his scream, or the <u>look he gave me.</u> The blood gushed in a stream. At first I intended to kill him. Cut up the body and take it home. But the weather was hot and I knew as I had no ice, it would <u>stink</u> and betray me. So I found cold water on his dickey then slowly found the rest of the Peroxide on the open wound. Then I took the rest of the vaseline in a clean handkerchief

them. My mouth fairly watered, to see what it would taste like. I always wanted to eat a boys nice fat ass. I also had a strong desire to cut off his prick and balls. Split them open, roast them and eat them. But I knew if I did that I would not have him to torture or be tortured by him. I pissed and shit all on him in his mouth - eyes - Ears. He did to me. I know we eat over 10 lbs of peanut butter and drank several gallons of cider, between us in the 5 weeks I had him. All things have an end. My job was finished and I could not afford to keep him. Realizing that I must go home. He did not want to put them on, but opened my pants, took out my dick and sucked me off. Then I was tempted I tied him up again, played with his dickey until it got stiff. Then I took the knife and sliced off half of it. I shall never forget his scream, or the look he gave me. The blood gushed in a stream. At first I intended to kill him. Cut up the body and take it home. But the weather was hot and I knew as I had no ice, it would stink and betray me. So I poured cold water over his dickey then slowly poured the rest of the Peroxide on the open wound. Then I took the rest of the Vasoline in a clean handkerchief

(Cook and eat entire body)

and bound him up. I untied him, put his clothes on the chair by the side of the bed. I gave him $10⁰⁰, kissed him good bye. Took first train I could got back home. Never heard what became of him, or tried to find out

God delivered Jacob and his people out of the hands of their enemies

He smote the Egyptians in their <u>Hinder Parts</u>. <u>His Command</u> is Spare not the Rod

<u>His Holy Book</u> Says <u>Purge Thyself of Sin</u> — <u>with the Rod</u>

The Jews stripped and whipped Jesus with switches, before they Crucified Him. Who am I, most unworthy of sinners that I should not be stripped and whipped?

Abraham offered up his own son as a Sacrifice to Almighty God

#9

and bound him up. I untied him, put his clothes on the chair by the side of the bed. I gave him $10.00, kissed him good bye. Took first train I could get back home. Never heard what become of him, or tried to find out

God delivered Jacob and his people out of the hands of their enemies

He smote the Egyptians in their Hinder Parts. His Command is spare not the Rod

His Holy Book says Purge thyself of Sin - with the Rod

The Jews stripped and whipped Jesus with switches, before they Crusified Him. Who am I, most unworthy of sinners that I should not be stripped and whipped?

Abraham offered up his own son as a sacrifice to Almighty God

(Remarks made by Mr. Fish while I read story. Taken down by Flo.)

"I didn't give him (Thomas) any thing to eat for 5 days. —
He was here 5 weeks altogether. — He didn't resist. Acted
just like a child 10 yrs. old." (NB: probably a defective).
"I done the same thing with myself — (set on fire).
Mr. Dempsey saw some of the marks here" (indicates his
posterior).

(How often come during these 5 wks?) A number of times
every day. When I was beating him."

"You can ask me about it after you read it, and see
how deeply it's impressed in my mind."
"I intended to kill him + cut him up completely. But it was
warm + I thought if I took the meat back it'd decompose +
people wd smell it. He gave me such an agonized look I didn't
kill him. & I can see it now (covers his eyes c̄ his hand,
+ pauses a few minutes). So I used peroxide first, then
tied it (penis) up so it wdn't bleed too much. I left
o $10. — bill in the chair 'kside him and left town. Pat's
the only one I ever ran away from."
"Was in 23 states. Montana was the farthest west. Lived
in there. Knew absolutely nothing about the McDonnell boy."

152

(Remarks made by Mr. Fish while [shorthand symbol] read story. Taken down by Flo.)

"I didn't give him (Thomas) any thing to eat for 5 days. -

He was there 5 weeks altogether. - He didn't resist. Acted just like a child 10 yrs old. ([shorthand symbol]: probably a defective).
"I done the same thing with myself - (set on fire).
Mr. Dempsey saw some of the marks here " (indicates his posterior).

(How often come during thee 5 wks?) A number of times every day. When I was beating him."

"You can ask me about it after you read it, and see how deeply it's impressed in my mind."
"I intend to kill him & cut him up completely. But it was warm & I thought if I took the meat back it wd decompose & people wd smell it. He gave me such an agonized look I cdn't kill him. I can see it now (covers his eyes [shorthand symbol, with] his hand, & pauses a few minutes). So I used peroxide first, then tied it (penis) up so it wdn't bleed too much. I left a $10.- bill on the chair beside him and left town. That's the only one I ever ran away from."

"Was in 23 states: Montana was the farthest west. Lived in them. Know absolutely nothing about the McDonnell boy."

<u>FISH</u>, <u>Albert</u>   Westchester County Jail II-12-35
                                    in People <u>vs</u> Fish

    64 years of age.

<u>P.H. & F.H.</u>   Father general business man. Pris. 12th child.
Fa. married twice. Died when def. was 5. Remembers how he
looked: was short, weighed 220 lbs.

            Mother died when def. 33. Like her more. Was
youngest child. Earliest memory: playing in the yard. At about
4 father called him 'Stick-in-the-mud'. Mother had position in
U.S. Treasury. Episcopalian.

            Def.: At 3 Dr. said he had St. Vitus' dance. 5 to 7
in orphanage. Mother took him home. Ran away every Saturday.
Very unhappy. Graduated public school at 15; not left back;
good marks. In grocery business while at school and later.
Painting trade begun at 17, two years after leaving school. Did
painting and decoration. Painter's cloic 3x yearly for last 20
years. Transient paralyses of right hand and foot. Dr. in
present jail talked about lead poisoning. Painted in Sanford
Hall, Flushing, L.I.; worked in mental sanitariums: Dr. Richard
Brown, 2 yrs., Dr. Coombes sanitarium in Corona, L.I. 2xyrxxx
8 mos.; and in other institutions. '

            1930: in Bellevue 1 month. Dr. Gregory wanted Kings
Park. Seen by a short, stout Italian. (Dr. Bromberg?) I think
so. Schilder asked only how I came to write those letters. I said
'a sort of mania'. Other patients told me what to say.'If they
say, country place, say no; that is K.(ings) P.(ark).' Fear of
being drugged "bugged". Other patients told him, Schilder only
asks about sex.

                            156

ARRESTS :   at 16, in Washington: cashing a forged check for $35.-
Discharged.

1903 (at 32) in L.I.: manager of a grocery store; embezzlement; took proceeds of several days; 1-5 State
Prison. Was in Sing Sing 16 months. No mental tests;
did not lose time.

1922 (at 52) false check for $67.- A & P store cashed
it; Made restitution. Charge reduced to petty larceny;
suspended.

1930 (at 60) check for $300.- also cashed by A & P
Store. Reduced to petty larceny. Suspended sentence.

1929 (at 59) sending obscene letters. Fed. Judge Knox.
Probation for 6 mos., to Bellevue.

1931 (at 61) same. Discharged home in custody of
married daughter. Kings County 3 weeks. Probably
Dr. Loughran. He did not spend much time with him.

Sex.   Married in 1898, on Feb. 5th. "That's when I married the

mother of my children. My firdt marriage. (Legally?) Yes.

Inthe Church of the Holy Communion.....

Before marrying his subsequent three wives, he told them

all what he wanted: "told them just what my inclinations

were: beating, urination, No.1, No.2, torture, and all.

I told my second wife my first wife was dead."

At 31, (391) missed women; masturbated; worried about xxyx

draxnixgxx it; does not remember why. No h,s. Daydream-

ing: imagine in homes, beating children (boys exclusively)

with whips.

First wife xixx living; had 6 children by me. Left me in 1917.

Left children in home , sold everything in the house; Youngest

child was 3 at that time. She now has 3 children more. Man was

a boarder. Intercourse once a night. After youngest child he

wanted no more children, she wanted more. x Cunnilingus and

penelictio. Hit her on behind every night. "She seemed well broke in when I got her." She was 19. She hit him on behind,too, with hand. She'd also take a switch. 'Liked it best when she hit me.' Youngest born in 1913 1913-1917 rarely with her. Never beating without intercourse.

Relations with boys and girls, 9, 10 years. Use them in rectum. Down on them and they on me. Cat houses: beat girls and they him. Colored and white. Girls of 10 in tb.home. It never came out. Always managed to cover it up. Children never seem to tell. Boys and girls under 14 - over a hundred. Always desire to hit them on behind. Mostly boys, but girls too. Raised welts and drew blood. In basements. Changed into overalls, put on over bare body. They never saw him in regular clothes. Gave the boys money. Very few girls. 25¢ Would draw blood, but they'd come back. Go down on them, and opposite. 'Prefer to have them go dpwn on me'. Dr. Lichtenstein got a lot of this. "If you ever get on a lunacy commission, I could help you".

Had boys and girls urinate on me; sprinkle on face now and then, but mostly on body and also in mouth. Cyril Quinn, he was 14 then, the last; That was about 10 yrs. ago. Something told me I eventually wd get into trouble. Hard time to control it, to overcome it.Girls too. Did xxx on boys in mouth, face and body; in basements. Never on a girl. No defecation with boys. -

Urinated on wife, and she on me, she in his mouth and she in his.
'She seemed to like it.'
Made boys do #2. on a piece of paper on the floor. 'I stick their
nose in it'. 'I made them take it in their mouth". For money.
'Let's play a game -- strip poker.'
Washington to N.Y. in 1894. Went on trips to Albany, Philadel-
phia, Boston, Bridgeport, Mass. etc. (Why not caught?) Luck.
Been all over the country.

In Washington at 17, before Wanderlust to N.Y. Nigger
boy of about 12. Sambo. Well built, ebony, Found an old boat
house onthe Potomac; kept him there a week. Did almost everything;
down on me; drink #1, eat #2, did same to him. I ate it from his
behind and he the same to me. He whipped me and I him. He bled
quite some. When he found he was well fed, he liked his stay.
(Then why captive?) I was afraid he'd ᵗʰᵃᵗ tell his mother. I
had to bring in switches. We'd wear them out with each other.
I kept him naked all the time he was there. I seemed to have a
desire to see him that way.

In Eastern *River* Home st 50; in basement paint shop,
the key fitted the storeroom. Several times a white boy there
(about 11 yrs.). Kept him for hours. Paid him.

In St. Louis, colored boy 15 in my room. Came to do
work for landlady. I got him in my room. I did exactly as with
the others. Hesitated first.

In Newark in 1927 in cellar. Boy of 9. Tried to do"it"
in his mouth. Hit him on behind, hard and he bled. He began to
holler. I hit with a stick. I changed my room. Left my satchel
in the room.

About five times that I had to run away. Did not tell in
Bellevue; they did not ask.

All boys, the oldest 16, the youngest 9. Lashed them with a
cat-o-nine tails. Had to run away from Bridgeport, Conn. Always
in cellars. Once up in a garret. Hit the 16 yr. old boy most.
Lashed him on back and penis. Drew blood from his back and a
little from his penis. I hag a handkerchief like a gag in his
mouth. Bit them in the behind, left marks with my txx teeth,
not that they bled. Some urinated on. About two of them he
tied hands and feet. Biggest one, I tied him.

Cut franulum of penis with scissors of a boy who was about
1B 10 or 11. Just seemed sort of a desire. To cut the whole
penis off was what was in my mind a number of times. That's what
was in my head with the Budd boy.

All my lifetime a preference for boys.

Early in life, Sunday school teacher Miss Wilkes wanted me
to study for the ministry. Religiously inclined. Great reader
of Bible.

Budd boy: I had sort of an idea through Abraham offering
his son Isaac as a sacrifice. It always seemed to me that I had
to offer
/ a child for sacrifice, to purge myself of iniquities, sins.
abominations in the sight of God. Such a Sodom and Gomorrha.
Christ seemed to appear in a vision night and day, mostly at
night. Saw almost the exact resemblance of it, the hands stretched
out. I woke right up and see it, as though he was there at the
bedside. I've seen his lips move. I couldn't exactly hear but

from the forms his lips took that he told me that this child (Grace) would eventually be outraged and tortured and so forth and that I should sacrifice her in order to prevent her future outrage. (means 'raping her'). Visions of Christ frequently. (First at about 14.) More frequent since my wife left me. First were shortly after my wife left me in 1917. (18 yrs.ago). I could vision my children in the rooms looking for their mother. Mostly in daytime-- broad daylight. Nights, too. Many times I have seen that. Before I began to see other things. Always in robes. Angels same way. Christ gave him command to kill Grace Budd. Wehn cutting frenulum, desire -- that was always a desire.

Hallucinations and delusions. I've heard voices speaking these things (exceppts from biblical verses). "Stripes" means to lash them, you know. I could hear words spoken, and of course a great deal I have read. I could put the words together and see what they meant. Such words like 'stripes', 'rewardeth', 'delighteth', then I made up the rest from what I had read.
(First time heard?) Soon after I began to torture myself with these needles, I'd say. About 10 yrs. ago. Voices told me to purge myself. (Where put the needles?) Up under the spins. I did put one in here too (scrotum) but I cdn't stand the pain. Only took out one needle. Cdn't get the others. Seemed I was told in a vision to purge myself of sin, by self-torture. That's what induced me to put them in. (Words without seeing things?) Mostly - quite frequently saw human body being tortured - some-one in Hell. Heard words alone too. Saw figure of Christ when heard "stripes", for instance, or "delighteth".

After I had that boy in the boathouse, I ~~had a boy~~ neet man on 14th St. ~~I was not bad looking~~ He took me to Toni Sarg Theater. After the show he rented a room at 95 ~~Broadway~~ Bowery. Was then 17. He had me strip, used me between 12 and morning about 4 times. Pecker in my mouth, kiss his behind, same to me. Often kissed behinds, boys , girls, wife. After doing #2. I to them, mostly.

I have nothing to live for. I have no particular desire to be killed. It is a matter of indifference to me. I do not think I am altogether right. (Crazy?) Not exactly. I compare myself a great deal to Harry Thaw, in his ways and actions and desires.

(What is Fusion?) I don't know. Sort of a third party.

Visions. In cell, visions of Christ. I really see it, just as you see pictures of the ascension. He appears in visions. I know he does not really come. That impresses me a good deal. Only time he told me something was Grace Budd. I see his lips move, but no message.

Imaginations: One Sunday in jail, Chinese asked me to write 2 letters, to his son and minister. Reaching for a blank sheet; a hand reached through the bars with a pistol in it. Albert Budd with a pistol in his hand. (When they brought prisoner to police headquarters, he tried to get at him·) Was scared. Asked the warden if he saw anybody there.

No voices. Ringing in ears. Hearing bad for about 5 yrs.,both sides. Very good hearing until 5 yrs. ago. Pupils over medium

162

wide; react promptly to light and accommodation. Slightly
limited excursion. No lead line on gums (Has no teeth). Paralyses
transient, even now; on right side: would drop things from hand
sometimes. Hand would feel numb, would rub them and be OK.
"Sometimes it caught me in the leg, especially since the needles."

Vavasour and Lambert: 8-11 at night. 27 needles in body. X-ray.)

Moody spells. Shortly after my wife left me. It hurt me in
every way, more for the children. Sent the children to the movies
and sold everything in the house.
(How long these gloomy spells?) Not long after my wife left me.)
They'd come at periods. Sometimes last a day, sometimes several
days. Don't answer, don't eat, don't drink. Nothing at all.)
Gloomy spell since here in jail. Didn't eat or drink. Warden
called the doctor who said,'This man is starving'to death'. (Why?)
I can't chew the meat. I haven't a tooth in my head. (In
such spells) can't listen to the radio sometimes at home. Cdn't
stand the least little noise. Grandchildren very disturbing. I'd)
just jump at the least little thing. Wd sit gazing into oblivion,
so to say. In midst of conversation, would forget entirely what)
I was talking about. Many times my oldest grandchild, Gloria,
would come in and remind me it was dinner time. She's a great
little dancer. She's 12 yrs old, in 7-A. I just idolized her -
my first grandchild. She's going to take stage dancing.

Read about Spanish inquisition. Joan of Arc- tortured
her and burned her alive. Guy Fawkes. Quo Vadis. Flagellation.
Had pictures. ~~Every~~ Every time I see anybody listed:e.g. whipping
in Delaware. Used them for masturbation. Had nudist pictures.

Unhappy here (weeps). Remorse for action in taking the
life of that child; my family, children and grandchildren.

Vision of Christ asking sacrifice three months before
act. Believes a "direct message". Believes girl would have been
raped eventually. "The only interpretation of it that I could
have was that she should be saved in that way."
Defloration: "I should judge 10 or 15 times". Girls 12 -
14. Hurts a little bit. "I always seemed to enjoy everything
that did hurt." I used to beat myself; made a paddle with tacks.
(Why not caught with children?) Luck.

Rejected lawyer Heisee whom son brought. "He didn't
seem to have ability." (Who understood you nearest?)
Italian doctor in Bellevue.

Prisoner speaks about a recent change in his life. "I did
not have those thoughts about harming children. Idea about
not harming children came since the Grace girl. " (Slipped?
" with boys mostly, but also ô girls. "(This was after the
appearance of Christ.)

2-15-35 (Spontaneously)

The police at the Tombs asked if I drank the girl's blood.
(^{D}r. Lichtenstein, etc.) I denied it and said it was all bunk,
but it was true. I drank about one or two swallows, good swallows,
and swallowed some. But I spat out most. It tasted sicken-
ing, nauseating. If I'd drank any more, I would have vomited.
I had that feeling.

I cut off all the flesh around her breast (just the beginning of a breast, she had) where her teat was, and the flesh
off some of her belly and legs, and all the meat I could get off
her abhind. I took it home (409 East 100 St.) I cooked it over
the gas stove, broiled it. I ate all of it, every bit of it.
Not all at once. It tasted to me like veal. I had other things
with it. (Onions, carrots and gravy). I got a hard one when I
ate it. I masturbated sometimes several times a night during the
days I ate it. I always had a desire to eat human flesh, ever
since I was told of cannibalism by my brother, the sailor, when
I was a boy. He saw it in China and in the Fiji Islands.(No
sexual things with brother, 11 years older,)

I intended to violate her. I took my clothes off. (I told
them so I wouldn't get blood on me, but that wasn't what I had in
mind. I was asked so many questions after I was arrested I
couldn't get my mind together.)   She picked flowers. I
stripped in the other room. I went to the window and called 'Grace'.
When she saw me naked she screamed and said, 'I'll call mama.'
I grabbed her by the throat and almost carried her in the room
and laid her on the floor and attempted to violate her. She
kicked and struggled. I had a hard one. I wanted to quiet her
first. She was losing consciousness and said 'kiss me' and

played three or four times with my pecker. I saw she suffered
from my strangulation. I placed my knee on her chest to squeeze
the breath out of her, to get her out of her misery. I intended
to violate her first and to beat her afterwards. She was too far
gone. She was practically gone. Right then I would have given
every drop of blood to bring her back to life. I intended to
violate her first and then switch her. I had some switches in her,
in her behind. (Not breast or between legs.) I always had in
mind only whipping, where I was whipped myself in the Home. I
didn't think she would put up such a struggle. She was a frail
looking child. She gave me the surprise of my life.

I intended to take the (Budd) boy, to cut his pecker off,
split it open, and then whip him on his behind. They asked if I
didn't think it was a fatal affair. I said that would be a fatal
affair. I intended to whip him until he bled. I would have
left the boy in the house, tied up, and gone back to my room,
packed up my things and left town.

I had another vision in the jail, about a week after I got
here. I woke up with a start. The guard had just passed at 2a.m.
I saw the same vision: her brother reaching in the same way with
a pistol in his hand. I jumped up with a start and yelled, and
asked Pat if there was anybody in the next cell. I knew the
cells were empty.

I drank the blood when I cut the head off. I had a
large painting pail, a 50 lb. paxx paint pot, that I had sand-
papered out clean. Most all that afternoon I had a hard one.
I come the first time when I was cutting the body up, the
second time on my way home. I came right in my pants while I
was carrying the meat, thinking of the child, how she looked in
life and what my intentions were. I got no pleasure out of
choking her to death.

(Nearest you came to killing?) I often in whipping
children had a desire to keep it up and whip them to death, as
I have read of such being done. Negro who had violated white
girls and then set them on fire. When I was in Eastern River
Home painting, I had a girl called Minna, 14. She was very
loose in her ways, although only a child. I had her and intended
to violate her and whip her; but what stopped me was the young
man who had a master key showing the empty flat. I put her in
a closet and put a 50lb. paint pail in front of the closet.
Otherwise I would have been in a fix right there. The manager
said he had heard things; he felt like kicking me out. He must
have heard things from some of these children, 20 yrs. ago.

At 17 I intended to eventually kill that colored boy
in Washington. I would have whipped him till he was unconscious
and then cut him up. alive. From reading the Peary expedition.
That's where I first got the desire to taste human flesh. I intended to cut off his pecker and privates, and split him open like
a sheep between the legs. Never ate human flesh before Grace.
Often had the desire to do so, but never the opportunity. The

The papers in Washington stated that in the Peary expedition three members of the crew had been eaten. It gave the details, the one who drew the shortest straw was chosen.

In 1929 at Dr. Lamb's on a Sunday afternoon away from the asylum I had a boy of 14-15. /I was leading him up there with the purpose to kill him and cut him up. I would have/ intended to first use him from behind and then /hit him on the head with a stone and then get the implements and cut what I wanted and leave the rest out there. A number of automobiles came along while I was still looking for the proper place. If it hadn't been for the passing autos, I would have killed him./

(Tied cases?) Tied hands behind back, and tied feet. I have done that many times -- 20 times or more. The one in St. Louis -- a colored boy on Olive Street -- I had him a long while. About 3 1/2 to 4 hours. First I stripped him naked, in a cellar. Then I used him from behind. Still had a hard one. He used me. We took it in the mouth. I whipped him on the behind. At first he liked it, then he began to scream. Tehn/I stuffed a handkerchief in his mouth. I really intended to kill him too, but I lost heart and left him there. I left the city./ There was some blood on his behind.

I tied the hands, not the feet, of probably half a dozen girls in different cities. Bridgeport. Always left city afterwards. Raised big welts, but drew no blood. Used to hit them on their behind, belly, breast and in between legs. Always had them gagged. (Killing?) It was more to torture than to kill. I have tortured myself with a paddle with nails.

(Are you guilty of the Gaffrey boy?) (Blushes.) " No." (Describes
identification in the Tomb. =

done

170

Often went to brothels. Kiss their behinds and between legs. Spank them a little, let them spank me. Most in Phila. Colored and white. Had desire to kiss behind clean. "I have kissed their behinds clean many times".

Third wife: I. wrote her that I wanted to eat her #2 and drink her #1 which I did, both. Her mother wrote me the same kind of letter that I wrote her. She drew a picture of #2 coming out of her behind into my mouth, and said I could have all the peanut butter that I wanted just as it came out fresh and hot.-

Was kicked several times by Detective-sergeant Fitzgerald in Police Headquarters, between the legs. I had not confessed then. I always had on my mind in the last three years that I had to confess. I realized that I'd never be able to do what I originally intended, carry the secret to my grave.

I never injured the other children seriously, but hurt them more than Grace. I enjoy the sensation of giving them pain. It always seemed to thrill me. I used to read of boys being circumcised. I always had a desire to do that. I did it a little bit on myself.

I just happen to think -- Once I was whipping a boy. I had him tied up, hands and feet, in my room. I had a handkerchief in his mouth. He was 14. He struggled before I tied him up. I sat on the bed. He lay across my lap. I told him I'd give him a dollar and that pacified him. After I spanked him on his behind, I took a piece of sandpaper, No. 2, pretty rough, and

rubbed the cheeks of his behind pretty roughly. /The desire to
inflict pain, that is all.that is uppermost.7 I come while he
was laying on my lap. In fact, a girl only had to sit on my lap
only a few minutes before I got a hard one. If she sat there
long I would eventually come. I had a razor blade in my room
and I slit between the cheeks of his behind-- one quick cut --
I had my mouth there and sucked the blood and swallowed it. That
was the only time before Grace that I swallowed blood. Even
beef blood I couldn't swallow.

Many times thought of cutting off boy's penis, but I never
got the opportunity.

Some places things must have come out after I left there.

(Youngest?) About 9. Boy. Only just fooling more than
anything else. Just rtying to stick it in his behind. I was
never built heavy like some men are.

6 children. 5 Grandchildren. In very poor circumstances.

Always very religious. /"Religion was one of my strong points".

/I have been in 23 states; had children in every state.7
Prostitutes have told me men wanted just to hit them, and not to
lay with them at all. Never whipped a woman older than 15 seriously.

Never did #2 on children, but often #1 all over them,-- in
mouth forcibly and all over. They splutter and spit it out. Not
to Grace.

(Grace?) /Murder was not in my heart at all. It never was.
I intended to use her. I was always soft-hearted and I loved
children./ When I left St. Ann's in N.Y. (I was sexton there
1920/21) the children cried because I was so nice to them.
Write the Rev. Harold G. Willis, West Orange, N.J., rector of
the Episcopal church there. I was also sexton of Bethany Memorial Church, N.Y.C. in 1923.

Never had temptation toward children.

At Orphanage from 5 to 7. (Animated) Some boys as
old as 14, youngest 3. I did it to them in the behind, they in
my behind. I did it to the girls. Sister Sarah (about 30) had
a cord with a hair brush and with a whip like a *riding whip* and a big
cross around her neck, a great combination (smiles). For the
least offense, laughing or talking, she'd take off our pants,
whip our bare behinds with the wooden part of the hair brush,
the whip or both. Often drew blood. Often in bath room, would
strip us completely naked and use whip on us. Toward latter
part of when I was there I got a hard one when she did it. I
know she enjoyed it. The bigger boys used to go in her room
late at night. I got excited mostly when she whipped me. In
order to escape whipping one learned how to lie. I got excited
when she whipped others, too, and sometimes 6 at a time. I used
to get a pleasure seeing their behinds get red under the spanking
they got. We were taught to beg. St. John's Orphanage. (Describes begging in boys in detail; very animated). Boys went
behind the fence, took things out. That's the way we learned how
to steal. That was before I went into public school. In other

173

words, I had a bad start.

Eating #2 in last 20 years. Take a girl who had done that and then clean her up. And then I seemed to acquire a taste for it. Sometimes I eat all that they done. At first it made me sick, several times so that I vomited. But then it did not do that. First with first wife, more with children ,and then with prostitutes. Mostly with children because/theirs wasn't so strong as a grown person's.

Needles: About 5 or 6 yrs. after my wife left me,- about 10 yrs. ago. Suffered for yrs. with rupture #x (talked about this a great deal to Dempsey). To relieve the pain I began to stick needles in these,-- first half way, then took them out again. Then enjoyed it and got like a kick out of it. There are 27 in my abdomen. That's what the X-ray shows. Got a hard one when sticking in the needles. Sometimes I come a little.

I'll never forget you, doctor.

Any case where mutilation or whipping was done always seemed to interest me.

Raped boys from behind, making them bleed,-- at least 10. All were gagged. Liked it that they bled. Often got kicked in shins or scratched, but liked that too. In fact, when I had to struggle for it I got more pleasure out of it. (How not caught?) Never went to same neighborhood again, or went to another city. Before doing that, always put on painter's overalls, a sort of disguise. So very few of them ever saw me in street clothes.

ALIASES: Frank Howard

John W. Pell

Robert Hayden

Thomas A. Sprague

"That's all."

Albert is not my right name. My real name is Hamilton Fish.
It was only when I left school, at 15, that I changed my name.
(1885) xx A distant cousin on father's side was ex-secretary
of state , a Hamilton Fish, under Grant. Now a Hamilton Fish
is a member of Congress from Garrison, N.Y., a descendant of
the ex-secretary. Changed my name to Albert long ago because
in school the boys called me Ham and Eggs and all that. Mother's
second child died with water on the brain. I took his name,
Albert. Father came from Augusta, Maine, a personal friend of
James G. Blaine, secretary of state under Garfield. Dr. Rayburn
my family physician, attended Garfield when he was shot. Some
members of my family are very wealthy, -- Leland Hotel owners;
Brown, - Herald Tribune under Gordon Bennett.

In Bellevue, they asked me about relations with boys, but I
denied it. Did not tell them anything about #1 or #2. The main
questions were why I wrote those filthy obscene letters.

Writes letter to Dempsey explaining in detail how beads
could not have been identified by Mrs. B. What held them there?
They were not there, head but off, etc.

Has implements in cell to mark himself. Writes lawyer to
bring doctor to see the marks. "Do you think that would be
a good scheme?" Writes lawyer: "God commanded me to purge myself of sin through torture and shedding of my blood. I
shall tell him (the dr.) I have been doing it once a month."

"I never mortally injured another soul, not even an animal."

Often spanked himself with hairbrush. I never could understand myself. I always had a desire to inflict pain on others
and to have others inflict pain on me."

When having relations with men, I like to see them stripped,
well-built with big behind. Have done everything. Never in love
with one. In love with wife No. 1 and No. 3, less with No.4.
All are living. Never got a divorce. I simply left one and
went to another. In 1930 I made a list out of the matrimonial
bureau. With all four did these things. They all enjoyed everything I did. I switched them and they switched me. They all
were over 40. One was 52.

He dates all from the Orphanage.

Never belonged to Nudist colony; interested; "anything naked always interested me."

Harry Thaw whipped girls, gave them $100.-

Vision of Christ was before the Grace Budd murder. Said sacrifice the boy as Abraham did Isaac. *Identify with God*

All they did in Bellevue was make me do mental gymnastics and puzzles out of wood, and asked me about these letters.

From 1928, before Grace, lived alone. I could not do these things with children in the house. Desire to whip became stronger at that time. That's why he left home. *(And daughter's statement in King's County chart.)*

(Worried?) Always afraid of developments.

Elmsford, N. Y.   Sept 18/32

Dear Madam

      I am a widower with two boys 12 & 14 I wish to board out.
I am a travelling man and want to find a nice clean home with a good
motherly woman who can take full charge of them and treat them
exactly as if they were her own.   I prefer a widow on a farm near a
school.   Since their mother died they have caused me a lot of trouble
by not going to school.   The Judge said to me if they were his boys
he would spank them good, twice a day for a month.   I have no time
nor any one to do it.   I want a woman who can and will use back of
hair brush (as my own mother did) and one who wont hesitate to strip
them and use a switch when necessary.   I am willing to pay a good
rate, but the boys must be cured of the habit.

      If willing let me hear from you

        I am yours very truly

              A. H. Fish

Envelope addressed:

      P. O. BOX 241

         Monsey

           N. Y.

FISH'S VILE LETTERS

"Once settled into a city or town, he had the habit of writing obscene letters. Not just at random. He would buy cheap magazines, with personal columns for the lovelorn (or would-be lovelorn) in them, or he would get names from matrimonial agencies. His obscene letters were not, on the whole, as incoherent as his life or behavior. They were to the point."
- Mel Heimer, *The Cannibal*

Letters written in the spring of 1929 in response to newspaper classified ads:

I wish you could see me now. I am sitting in a chair naked. The pain is across my back, just over my behind. When you strip me naked, you will see a most perfect form. Yours, yours, sweet honey of my heart. I can taste your sweet piss, your sweet shit. You must pee-pee in a glass and I shall drink every drop of it as you watch me. Tell me when you want to do #2. I will take you over my knees, pull up your clothes, take down your drawers and hold my mouth to your sweet honey fat ass and eat your sweet peanut butter as it comes out fresh and hot. That is how they do it in Hollywood.

[Bobby] does not wet or muss his clothes or the bed. He will tell you when he has to use the toilet, #1 or #2. For #1 his pants must be unbuttoned at the crotch and his monkey taken out. His pants and drawers are all made with a drop seat. All you have to do is loose three buttons in the back and down they come. Saves a lot of undressing. Handy when you want to spank him, just drop the seat of his pants and drawers. You don't have to strip him except at night for bed, or to give him a bath (or a switching). The Doctor says three or four good spankings a day on his bare behind will do him good as he is nice and fat in that spot. It will be an aid to him. When he don't mind you, then you must strip him and use the Cat-o-nine tails. Say you won't hesitate to use the Paddle or Cat-o-nine tails on him when he needs it.

September 30, 1934

My Dear Miss Shaw

I am a widower with a son of 19 who is a semi invalid. I am a director in the movies and must be back in Hollywood California by Oct 15. Before I go I wish lo see him placed in competent hands in some good private home. One that does not look or smell like a Hospital or institution. I am well able and quite willing to pay a good price for Bobbys care. But my instructions must be carried out. Here is the case —

When 5 he fell down the cellar stairs. Sustained a brain concussion. Has never been really normal since. Tho going on 20 good looking well built, fully developed. He has the mentality of the age when he fell. Every part of his body has grown but the brain. He is harmless and just so easy to spank or switch as a child of 5. When 12 he had an attack of infantile paralysis. He can walk, run, jump. Get in and out of the bath tub alone. No lifting to do or wheel chair to push. He has very little use of his hands or arms. Has to be washed,
dressed, undressed, given a bath. Rubbed all over daily with alcohol and assisted in the toilet. He gets cross and cranky at times, dont always mind. I am trying out European treatment in such cases. Prof Cairo of Vienna Austria, recommends it. He says when he gets a spell he must be whipped. They are having great success over there in cases like it. So you see as his own father I would sooner have him whipped any how then have him lose his reason entirely. Should you take him in charge on the first occasion he shows temper spank him soundly as you would a small boy and dont hesitate to use The Cat-o-nine-tails on his bare behind when necessary.

If interested, state your terms and when you can receive him. He is now in Phila in charge of a colored woman I have known 25 yrs. She says whipping is the best medicine she ever used.

I will call on you

Sincerely yours
Robert E. Hayden

October 2, 1934
My Dear Mrs. Shaw

Just got home and found your letter. Am so glad you are interested. Before I call on you, will you kindly advise me — Are you a widow? and if so would you consider another mariage? Will the presence of your daughter in your own home, prevent you from taking care of my son? You know there are some women who think it immodest, to strip a boy naked who is over ten years unless he is their own son. I know you are not ashamed to strip, bathe, rub, spank and switch my son or you would not have answered my letter. However I shall feel much more at ease if you will say you are not in your next letter. Would phone but dont hear very well. Will call on you as soon as I get your answer.

Yours very truly
R. E. Hayden

October 4, 1934
My Dear Mrs. Shaw

Just got your very nice letter. I am much pleased to know you are not one bit ashamed to strip Bobby Naked and bathe him. Am also glad you spoke to your daughter and she is willing to aid you in taking care of him. There is no reason why either of you should be. You know times have changed and so have people. What in times past was considered immodist is now very common place. Then again look at what young girls training to become Nurses - See and Touch in Hospitals. Bare in mind that it is for Bobbys own good that he is to be whipped. So dont let your heart stay your hand. Do you know that I feel that in part I am to blame for the condition Bobby is in. My conscience says that for being careless I should be whipped, in same manner (and place) you will whip Bobby. Some day I hope you will be able to accomodate me. I would give a nice new $100.00 bill for a good old fashioned spanking and a taste of the switch — once again. There is a place on 42 St called Fleishmans Baths where naked men are rubbed all over by women. White — Black — Chinese. Most women would get a kick out of spanking a naked man. But I prefer some privacy — in a home. Am a 33 D. Mason and will be busy next two days. How about
Sunday afternoon or night. Let your daughter read this letter. I am a man of the world and she can get knowledge of the world thru it.

I feel that we shall be fast friends.

Sincerely yours
Robert E. Hayden

New York Sunday Oct 7, 1934

My Dear Mrs Shaw

I have been called to Phila on some very important business. While there I shall make arrangements to have Bobby transferred on here and will then turn him over to you and your daughter for his treatment when you are ready for him. I have paid for his board and care up to Oct. 15. You see I am never sure just where I will be until Dec. 31-34 when my contract expires. I have always made it a custom to pay several weeks in advance. Now in your letters you have made no mention of your financial condition. You may be short of funds. If you are, dont hesitate to say so. You can give me your answer thru Mr Pell the bearer of this and I will then advance you as much as you may require. Mr James W. Pell is a friend and Ward of mine. He has been declared (incompetent) and I have $32,500 of his money in trust. He had a nervous break down and was in a nearby Sanitarium for 21 weeks at $100.00 a week. He is without a living relation and I dont see why you cant take him and so earn some of his money as well. Two of his sons were blown to pieces in the War. At times he imagines he is a boy at School, has been naughty and must be spanked for it. Dr Lamb said to Humor him — let him be a boy all over again and spank him. He gets short of breath and is subject to fits, when in water. For that reason he must never take a bath alone. The least I have in mind is this. You have told me that I need not worry about you being ashamed to strip Bobby naked and spank his bare behind. If you are not ashamed of Bobby you wont be of Jimmy. One bare behind is the same as another. Take him upstairs, undress him, give him a bath then spank him good. He will say teacher whip me. I shall not leave for Phila until Jimmy returns with your answer. Hope some day you will call me by my first name.

How about ———————————— my spanking???

Do I get it???   Oh—I—hope—so

Sincerely Yours
Robert E. Hayden

Monday October 8, 1934

My Dear Mrs Shaw

I had a friend of mine drive Mr. Pell or (Jimmy) to Little Neck. They stopped at Little Neck
Pkway and asked a policeman where your street was. They spent nearly an hour walking up one street and down another. It was so dark they could not see the numbers. Some one told them of a Mr. Chas Shaw an Electrical Engineer and a Dr Shaw but Jimmy got tired out. When I returned home I found him all in. He had the other letters with him and was all set for a good old fashioned spanking from both of you. That is of course when the (Mr) is not at home. You can arrange that. I shall be in Phila for a day or two. May go to
Washn D.C. before I return. Meanwhile you can write me, Belleview Stratford Pa and if you are ready for Jimmy, write him at the same address In N.Y. City.

I am very sincerely Yours
Robert E. Hayden

P.S. In 1928 Mr Pell operated on for a Hernia. When you have him stripped, you will see the mark of the incision. Look on his left groin, from his Penis to his hip bone. He was prepared for another operation ten days ago. All hair shaved off. That is why he looks like a picked chicken. He was found to have a bad heart, so it was called off. When you or your girl spank him, dont use your hand. If you have not a paddle, use the back of a hairbrush or get a few switches. There must be plenty of them near your home. I know Jimmy would give you a $100.00 bill for a good sound spanking. So I shall take it out of his money for you so spank spank spank. Harry K. Thaw gave $100.00 bills to girls for a spanking. Only he done the spanking on the girls bare behinds. He met them at the Staqe Door. Took them to his room at the Astor House, stripped them naked, turned them over his knee and used a Paddle. Many of them came 2 and 3 Times a week – to be spanked and get that $100.00 Show me a girl who is nice and has some modesty, but not too much. It dont pay your rent or taxes or buy the baby shoes. Out in Hollywood Laura La Plante came in my office dressed in her birth day suit and sat in my lap. We have an old Romany Gypsie woman who tells all the girls that if they can catch a man naked in his home, whip his bare behind with switches and then kiss him, she will surely marry him. Now they all carry switches.

Jimmy has a habit of painting his behind red or in Gold. When you strip, him you will see. I have told him just what to expect at your home. He is pretty tough don't be shy or slow in laying it on his behind. Limber up your arms for Bobby and his Daddy.

Robert

New Yok October 24, 1934

My Dear Mrs. Shaw

You have struck the nail on the head at last. You have been too modest. Take 100 women and give each the same chance I gave you and 99 of them would have jumped at it.

Bobby is still in Phila in the charge of the same colored woman, I am paying her $50.00 a week. It is not a question of price but— Service. He seems to like colored people and 1 have found that colored women and girls enjoy the job of spanking and switching a Naked white boy or man. Especially is it so with the girls regardless as to their age or size. There are many things about Bobby of which I have never written. Not because of modesty but because I well knew you would find out. I may as well speak of it now. He has such a strong tendency to play with himself (Mastibation) that I have been advised to have him
Altered or Sterelized.

Now as to Mr Pell or Jimmy. He is not a bit Looney. His Hobby is to be whipped, whipped, whipped. I wanted you to try your hands out on his bare behind just as a sample of what Bobby Would get.

He could come to your home and be stripped, well spanked and switched. Put on his

185

clothes and return to me. He is able to do so. Now if the Mr is at home in the evening, it would embarass both of you. But it can be done in the day time any hour you say. Take him to the house -- and go to his bare behind with a will. Now my dear I think I deserve the same — don't you think so??? I have the money to pay for it and am not stingy. So any hour and day you say for Jimmy Daddy — later — on. Now you just drop Modesty and speak Plain.

Robert

P.S. I can almost hear the smacks on Bobbys bare behind as those colored girls spank him. Your turn next

----

October 24, 1934
My Dear Mrs Shaw

Just now I am so busy I scarcely got time to really enjoy a good meal and wish you had room for the Daddy as well as for the son. I know I would enjoy some good home cooking with the prospects of a good Spanking now and then thrown in.

I have a sort of an idea that you and the (Mr) do not pull so well together. I would Just LOVE to give you a Royal good time and am capable of doing it, without his knowing of it. When I wrote you last of Spanking Jimmy, he had just been shaved for an operation and looked like a picked chicken. Now the hair is beginning to grow again. He has a strange habit of putting on his underwear backward. So you will no doubt find it that way when you strip him. Both of you warm his behind until it is good and red — all over. He will come down on the bus from Flushing and have a letter from me to you in his hand, so you know him. Black Coat— Grey Fedora. Have your daughter meet him. Once you have him in your home, upstairs I am sure both of you know—what —to— do. How about Sunday 2-4 P M for him? Have you a nice heavy Paddle??? Have you a nice Cat-o-nine-tails? You see there are three behinds to be spanked and switched. So now dont be — bashful. Dont be — modest Either of you Just say — Yes — Robert (Dear x if you want x You shall get a — plenty)

Until 1 hear from you — by by

Robert xxx
P.S. if Jimmy kicks or puts his hands in the way when you spank him — tie his hands

----

New York City October 29, 1934
My Dear Mrs Shaw

Mr Pell gave me your note.

He says you were afraid that in spanking him he might have a heart attack. I am taking him at 2 P.M. today to Roonoake Va. and turn him over to a man and wife who formerly lived in Washington D.C. (His old home) I shall then return to that city for a few days and then go to Phila. Bobby seems to get on well with colored people so I shall put him in charge of a widow who has a son of 27. Am beginning to think he really does need a man to care for him. Especially the parts that are so — very personal

Thanking you for the interest you have shown
Letter to Grace Shaw, November 9, 1934

My Dearest Darling Sweetest Little Girlie Grace

Just got your letter calling me dear Robert. Dear Honey Heart of mine, you have captured me. I am your Slave and everything I have is yours. Prick — Balls — Ass and all the money you want. . . . If you were my own sweet wife, you would not be afraid of me. 0 girlie of my heart would I love you — and how. Hug-Kiss-Squeeze you, spank you, then KISS just where I spanked! Your nice-pretty-fat-sweet ass. . . . You won't need toilet paper to wipe your sweet pretty fat Ass as I shall eat all of it, then Lick your sweet ass clean with my tongue.. . .

November 21, 1934

Dear Madam

I am a widower with 3 boys, 13-15-19 I wish to board out until the two youngest are thru
school. I want good plain food clean beds, sew mend darn and do their laundry. I prefer a widow, who has a girl old enough to aid her. Henry and John have caused me a lot of trouble by not going to school. . . . Their principle Miss Bruce said to me, if they were her boys, she would spank both of them soundly 3 times a day for a month and give John a dose of the Cat-o-nine-tails at bed time. She blames him most so do I. I have no time to do this and besides I think whipping children is a woman's job. I want a good motherly woman, who can and will assume full charge of the 3 boys. Make them obey you and when they dont take down their pants and spank them good. Dont hesitate to strip them to the skin and use the Cat-o-nine-tails on them, when you think they need it. Robert is feeble minded due to a fall. Tho going on 20, well built and strong he is much easier to spank or switch than Henry. He kicks like an army mule when being spanked. I want a woman who will whip any one of the 3 or all 3 at once if they need it. Our own doctor says if Bobby is not
spanked and switched when he gets cranky he is apt to lose his reason entirely. So he must be spanked as well. He is now in Phila Pa in charge of a Colored woman I have known 25 years. She has a daughter 17 and between them he is getting plenty of the paddle and Cat-o-nine-tails. Henry and John are in Upper Darby Pa in charge of two

189

Maiden Sisters, both ex School Teachers. They conduct a boarding school for boys and girls up to 17 yrs. Both are very strict and any boy or girl who misbehaves is spanked in front of the entire class. John is a big boy for his age and it shames him to have his pants taken down and be

spanked in front of a lot of girls. I want a place where all 3 can be together. ... I am willing to pay you $35.00 a week for the 3 boys, $15.00 a week extra when I am there. But if you take them you must assure me you will Use the paddle and Cat-o-nine-tails freely on all 3 boys. I want a woman who will not be embarrassed in stripping Bobby any more than Henry and John. So if you are interested tell me how to reach your place by car.

A. H. Fish

LETTERS WRITTEN BY FISH AFTER HIS ARREST

1351 - 3 Ave   New York City   Nov 11 - 34

Mr. Vincent Burke

    Dear Sir

        I was formerly a member of the Out-Door
Club, Tacoma Park Washington D. C. a Nudist group. Business
took me away/ I have travelled a lot so gave up my membership
in club. I am located here now permanently and wish to know
where you have your nudist meetings and the hours
        Hoping to be informed

          I am very truly

            James W Pell

Jan 15 1935

Dear Warden

When I was a free man, I dont every honest thing a man
could do in order to provide for my family.   Even in jail as you
know from reading my letters I have dont my best, to aid them. I
have not asked them to send me a penny or fruit or candy.   Not
even to call and see me.   Not because I did not want to see them
but because I know it is an expense they cant afford. Here is
one favor I ask of you.   Mrs. De Marco my youngest daughter now 31,
has been a Heart patient of Bellevue Hospital N. Y. C. past 11 yrs
and still is. On acot of her weak heart I hope she dont call.
Should she do so however before you call me have the M. D. look
her over and give her a stimulent or dont allow her to see me. I
am afraid of the effect it will have on her.   When I was in Bellevue
Hospital I dont my best to prove to Dr. Gregory that I was sane.
I have never tried to make any one think otherwise.   The M. D.
says to me dont worry.   All my children tell me the same.   I
always done all the worrying for the family.   I will never stop
until the end.   That end I shall do my very best to expedite.
My family dont even answer my letters.   I am thru, what have I
to live for.   Good - treatment means nothing to me now so I dont
want any. Any how a man with no teeth in jail is better off dead.
I have lived my life am old weak tired out

Thanking you for your kindness

I am very truly

A. H. Fish

Jan 13 - 35

Dear Warden

         I told you the truth as to what you would find in Stones
cell. Had I not been transferred I never would have known. He
showed me, told me just what he intended to do. It was from him I
got the idea in my head to do away with myself. Breakfast was late
today and Stone raved - cursed you and everybody about the place.
He used the vilest, most rotten language I ever heard come out of a
mans mouth. This P. M. he called Mr. Fowler a four eyed S of a B
and a lot of filthy names and threatened him. Passing his cell while
exercising I heard him mumbling to himself as to what he would do.
For some reason he has taken a dislike to Mr. Fowler and I think
it unsafe for a man of his age, to come inside the cage when he is
out. Everything I have told you or any who have spoken to me is
the truth. The cell I am in now is nice and light but I cant stand
Stone. I cant read my Bible with a man man raving - cursing -
swearing. Cant you put him down at the other end in # 1   When
my lawyer Mr. Carl J. Huyser was here 1 st he asked me when I was
in court and was asked if I had a lawyer to say I would like to have
him. When the Judge asked me - I simply could not open my mouth
to plea or say a word. Then he stepped up and plead not guilty for
me.   I have since then written the Dl A. and asked him to call
the attention of the trial Judge and have him assign him.   However
if you will drop a line to the D. A. I will thank you. Now I have
only $1.20. That I would like to use for newspapers. I would
like 5 stamps. What might of happened with such things in the
hands of a wild man like Stone. Now in telling you what I did
I hope I did you some good

              I am very truly

                        A. H. Fish

P. S.   Drop a Postal card to Mr. Carl J. Huyser and ask him to
        call and see me

East View N. Y.   Feb 6 - 35

Postmaster

    Dear Sir

        I was born at Washington D. C. and had a
brother by the name of Edward F. Fish.   I have not seen
or heard of him in over 20 years.   The last place I
know of that he lived was 40 F St N. W.   I am in great
trouble now and request you to try and locate him for
me.   If he is still living he is 67 and would be in
Washington.

        Hoping to hear from you at an early date
        I am very truly

                        Albert H. Fish

Elmsford N. Y.   Sept 22   [1935?]

Mrs. Robt Silonberg

    Dear Madam

         I received your very nice ;etter and from the way you
write of yourself, also of your home. I think I have found a place for
the boys. A nice clean home good contry air. Good plain food   I
also think from your training your own three sons, mine will get just
what they need. Many a good spanking and plenty of switching as well.
Now as I do not intend to let them see N Y City again until they are
18 except to go shopping. Who ever takes charge of them now, will
have them 3 or 4 years. Let us get aqquainted. My own mother died
when I was 9.   Dad married again. A woman 20 yrs younger than he.
She was a country school teacher. There were 5 of us four boys - one
girl. She was a real step Ma O.K. For the least ghing, she stripped
us naked and used dads riding whip on us. She stripped me and used
the whip when I was 17 for going to a dance New Years eve. I ran away
from home. Robert or 'Bobby' as you will call him was 14 May 19
Eugene or 'Gene' was 12 July 20 Both are good looking well built
boys especially Bobby I did not tell you half of what took place in
Cou t. But now as you are likely to be their Mama I want you to
know. The Judge was going to send them to a Reform School for bad
boys where the Matron and her assistants whip the boys severely some
of them 2 and 3 times a day. There is a new law now in effect. On
acct of jails being so full young men upto 21 yrs of age are classed
as boys and sent to the reform school. All are treated alike. There
is a big table in the laundry boys 18 - 19 - 2o are taken there by
the Matron Miss Phipps - stripped to the skin, made lay on the table
face down while she lashes them until blood is drawn. So you need not
be one bit backward in stripping Bobby and Gene as naked as the day
they were born and switching their bare behind - good and plenty
In fact my dear friend I had to promise the Judge I would strip and
whip Bobby at least twice a day for 30 days to save them both from the
reform school, where they would get it.   I would sooner have them
whipped by you in your own home. So you see how things are. I hope
you will dod it for me, as well as for the boys own good. There was
a colored woman in court they day I was there with the boys. She
spoke to me of taking them. Then wrote me a letter. I am sending
you a copy of it so you can see what she said.   So you see I cant
let any one have them, unless they send me a letter and promise me
they will strip the boys and span and switch their bare behind.
Bobby he blames most as he is the oldest and you must whip him twice
a day before and after school. I want a real mother ?   ?   ?
Give them a bath once every week. Dont let them jump and splach
water in bath room.   Gene is a holy terror on facets I remember.
A good spanking will teach him how to act. I am very glad the school
is so near. I want your letter to show the judge. So you write me
just what you will do to the boys speak plain for he said strip them
and use a cat o nine tails on their bare behind As to your rate I
am well able and willing to pay $25.00 a week but I must get service.
I also want to show Bobby what mama h s waiting for him - a nice big
bunch of switches and a big paddle. He is a good sized boy for 14
and is modest for a boy. No doubt he will be much ashamed when you
first strip and whip him, but boys soon get over shame. In order to
get aqquainted and make them feel at home, I would suggest that as soon
as I turn them over to you in your own home you take both of them to
the bath room, strip them give them a bath then a good S W I T C H I N G
Both of them know they are to get it good and plenty. Dont let your
Heart stay your hand.   They are just the right age to be well whipped

whipped.   I cant get away Before Sunday week but send me your letter
at once   so I can show the Judge the boys are in good hands and
will be spanked - well switched.   We will come by car as I can
bring their baggage.

              Sow now let me hear from you

                   I am yours very truly

                   Mr. A. H. Fish

I am sure you never raised your three sons without spanking and
switching them, bathing them many times.   Now you must handle mine.
I will pay four weeks board cash in advance and when I am on the
road will send a U. S. money order.   I will board at your home
when I am home from a trip

              We will talk things over

Envelope addressed

         Mrs. Robert Silonberg

              Monsey

P. O. Box 241   N Y

354 Hunter Street
Ossining, N.Y.

Mr. James Dempsey,   Jan. 9th 1936
105 So. Division Street,
Peekskill, N.Y.

Mr. James Dempsey
   Dear Sir:-

          Now that my case if off your hands- after a
long and ardurous battle on your part. Let me thank you -
which I do believe me from the bottom of my heart. Not so
much for my own sake - tho life is sweet to all of us -
regardless as to our age. However I thank you most of all
for my childrens and grand childrens sake. There is no man
living who could have done better than you did under the
circumstances and conditions you had to fight against. To
begin with - There is my own several confessions. That alone
left you no grounds to fight on - except the one you chose.
Had I known any letters I wrote was being copied while I was
in jail - then of course it would of have been different. The
letters I wrote my children convinced the jury I was sane that
slid the only prop us had to stand on - from under our feet.
Now added to that - instead of one man to fight you had no less
than '14' - Judge - D.A. - and the jury. It was not that they
were against you -they started out from the very first to get me.
Had I kept the secret a few yrs longer - the result I think would
have been different. You see it was brought to light at a bad
time - through a number of such cases in a short space of time-
the country was aroused. I have heard a number up here 'among the

                            -1-

officers' say that if You had had the case in N.Y. City you would have beat it. Now the next thing - when you get time - is to obtain the story of my life. Dr. Moore had it on his desk -- so when I was before the Lunacy Board, He asked me a number of questions regarding it. Thru it I am sure you can raise money that both my children and you as well can use. When you have read it then get in touch with some newspaper - or a popular magazine. You might also try the movies - it could be re-written and dramatized. There is excellent ground work for a Drama. Most of it - is actual facts just as they occurred from the days in the orphanage - all thru my life in 22 States -upto that fatal day. Such a life History put in action - played by competent actors and placed before the Public would bring in an abundent return to those who financed it. There is no part of the U.S. that my case has not been read and talked of. That old house is History now. Such a play as could be made of it - would draw the public like a house on fire. True Story is a good magazine - but I think the real money would be in the movies. The Fox Film Co.-Columbia - M.G.M. are the ones who would be most likely to produce such a play. Why not try your luck? Get in touch with several of them and of course- play for the best offer you can get. Allow them to use your name as my attorney - what an add for you. Now about the copies you spoke of - that is a master stroke. Get a number of them. Keep one for yourself and send me one. I can use it - as ground work- a foot hold - in the years before me. The papers you mentioned reaches more real people than any other I guess in the U.S.

-2-

However, the subject may not appeal to the City Editor - as a first
page display. There are of course other high class ones -to whom
such a piece of news will appeal and who would be only too glad to
publish same. Before you forget that I am in existence any longer
there is a matter I would ask your opinion on. I am charged in
N.Y. County with kidnapping now both parents testified in Court-
that their child left their home on June 3/28 -with their permission.
That is an undisputed fact. Is that - kidnapping? Then their is
that Murder charge against me - the McDonald boy somewhere in
Staten Island in 1924. The indictment was found in 1935 - '11 yrs after'
the body was found on the assertion of a man and his wife that I was
the same man - they ......up in a garage near their home. I done
one job in Port Richmond in 1916. At that time my wife and I were
living with our 6 children in College Point, N.Y. a long ways from
S.I. I can prove an absolutely good alibi -from the fact that in
1924 I was Sexton of Berthony Memorial Church - First Ave. & 67tSt.
Rev. Albert Brandeman was the pastor. He was the one who was
paralized and I and another man - had to carry him from his rooms
into the church -......3 flights of stairs then back to his rooms.
He is now dead and can not testify in my behalf. However the fact
that I was Sexton of that church-at that time - is a matter of
record in the church books. Wages were $25. a week and were paid
every Monday. Rev. Brandeman -paid all bills and kept the books.
Now Mr. Dempsey I ask you - in your knowledge as a lawyer and your
experienc e as an ass't D.A. can an indictment found on such flimsy
testimony hold? The assertion that I woke up in a garage was made

-3-

in Homicidal court - in a side room - where I was questioned by
D.A. Kelly of Richmond County. If I were a simple man and a
bum - it might hold good - but not in my case where I had a cosy
home - a wife and 6 children. At any rate their are two Warrants
here against me - as if I was not in trouble enough. One is for
Murder -other for kidnapping. To be charged with a thing I know
nothing of much less guilty of is a constant cause for worry on my
part. The charge was made a few days after my arrest and was only one
of several they tried to pin on me. I have told my children not to
believe what they saw in the papers about my being an Ogre -that
the only child I ever harmed bodily was the one for whom I am now
being punished. I am confident they do believe me - but at the
same time I would like to see those two indictments set aside-quashed.
One of them is a Duplicate of the charge that brought me here -the
other is -groundless. Later on in this year thru my children I
may get Mr. Carl Huyser of Port Jefferson to interest himself
in my behalf. It would be a great relief both to my children-grand
children and myself to see the cloud that hangs on us all removed,
and people know that I am not so black as painted. Thanking you
again for your efforts in my behalf and hoping you may get many
cases - but none as tough as mine was I am Very truly

                                    Albert H. Fish 90272

P.S. Write me now and then -when you have time.

                              -4-

FISH ADMITS HE MURDERED BILLY GAFFNEY

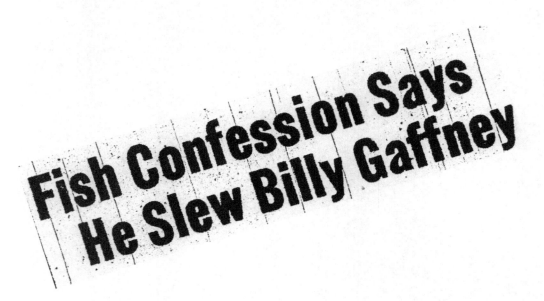

Fish Confession Says He Slew Billy Gaffney

BILLY GAFFNEY CONFESSION LETTER

Letter written after the trail by Fish to his attorney, James Dempsey.

There is a public dumping ground in Riker Avenue, Astoria. All kinds of junk has been thrown there for years.

Here is my plan: some years ago I lived at 228 E. 81, top floor front. Suppose I confess to you that I did_____ the Gaffney boy. In same manner I did the B girl. I am charged with the crime anyhow and many really believe I did. I will admit the motorman who positively identified me as getting off his car with a small boy, was correct. I can tell you at that time I was looking for a suitable place to do the job.

Not satisfied there, I brought him to the Riker Ave. dumps. There is a house that stands alone, not far from where I took him. A few yrs. Ago I painted this house for the man who owns it. He is in the auto wrecking business. I forget his name but my son Henry can tell you, because he bought a car from him. This man's father lives in the house. Gene, John, Henry helped me paint the house. There were at that time a number of old autos on the road.

I took the G boy there. Stripped him naked and tied his hands and feet and gagged him with a piece of dirty rag I picked out of dump. Then I burned his clothes- Threw his shoes in the dump. Then I walked back and took trolley to 59th Street at 2 am and walked from there home

Next day about 2 pm, I took tools, a good heavy cat-o-nine tails. Home made. Short handle. Cut one of my belts in half, slit these half in six strips about 8 inches long. I whipped his bare behind till the blood ran from his legs. I cut off his ears, nose, slit his mouth from ear to ear. Gouged out his eyes. He was dead then. I stuck the knife in his belly and held my mouth to his body and drank his blood.

I picked up four old potato sacks and gathered a pile of stones. Then I cut him up. I had a grip with me. I put his nose, ears and a few slices of his belly in grip. Then I cut him through the middle of his body. Just below his belly button. Then thru his legs about 2 inches below his behind. I put this in my grip with a lot of paper. I cut off his head, feet, arms, ands and legs below the knee.

This I put in sacks weighed with stones, tied the ends and threw them into the pools of slimy water you will see all along road going to North Beach. Water is 3 to 4 feet deep. They sank at once.

I came home with my meat. I had the front of his body I liked best. His monkey and pee-wees and a nice little fat behind to roast in the oven and eat. I made a stew out of his ears, nose, pieces of his face and belly. I put onions, carrots, turnips, celery, salt and pepper. It was good.

Then I split the cheeks of his behind open, cut off his monkey and pee-wees and washed then first. I put all in a roasting pan, lit the gas in the oven. Then I put strips of bacon on each cheek of his behind and put in the oven. Then I picked four onions and when meat had been roasted about one quarter hour, I poured about a pint of water over it for gravy and put in the onions. At frequent intervals I basted his behind with a wooden spoon. So the meat would be nice and juicy.

In about two hours it was nice and brown, cooked through. I never ate any roast turkey that tasted half as good as his sweet fat little behind did. I ate every bit of the meat in about four days.

His little monkey was as sweet as a nut. but his pee-wees I could not chew. Threw them in a toilet.

XXXX

You can put my children wise as to the above and if necessary put me on the stand.

I can relate the details just as if I were talking about the weather.

The place I have described is just such a one to do an act of this kind. How about calling in
several reporters and tell them that I told you God told me to purge myself of this sin and depend on his Mercy? Lead them down to the dump. They will bite hard. What a sensation. Gene, John, Henry, who worked with me on the house nearby can tell of same. Or do you think I ought to call in Father Mallet of Grace P.E., Church, White Pl. and confess to him? Then you let it loose.

Write down just what you want me to do. If it will be of any good, you can get my record from prison office. It shows emergency call about v P.M.; Cell l-B-14, Warden Casey and dr. (symptoms of lead poison).

While in Police Hdqurs., Dec. 13-14, had not as yet made confessions to any one. When officer F. W. King left room I was kicked hard in my stones as I sat in a chair, by Sgt. Fitzgerald. I can point him out to you in court. He said to me, even tho you are an old man, if you don't come clean, I'll take you downstairs and use a length of rubber hose on you. You take at least one shot at him in court for me.

Get torture paddle I made from officer King. He has it. Shows state of mind. Board with tacks driven thru it.

PART IV: THE TRIAL

9 JURORS CHOSEN FOR TRIAL OF FISH

House Painter Accused of the Murder of Budd Child Is Sullen at Opening Session.

SANITY TO BE CHIEF ISSUE

Talesmen Warned on 'Sordid' Testimony—Counsel Clash in Examining Panel of 70.

In the Name of the People of the State of New York:

TO Dr.Frederick Wertham,N.Y.C.N.Y.

You are commanded to appear before the SUPREME COURT of the County of Westchester, at the Court House, in the ~~City~~ of White Plains, in said County and State, on the 18th day of March 19~~35~~ , at nine o'clock in the forenoon, as a witness in a criminal action prosecuted by the People of the State of New York against Albert H.Fish

city

Dated at the ~~Town~~ of White Plains, Westchester County, N. Y., the 15th day of March one thousand nine hundred and Thirty-Five

{L. S.}

Bernard H.Koch
County Clerk of Westchester County.

DR ADOLPH SCHULTZ
DEPT OF ANATOMY
JOHNS HOPKINS HOSPITAL
BALTIMORE MARYLAND

WOULD YOU BE WILLING TO EXAMINE BONES ALLEGED TO BE THOSE OF

A MURDERED GIRL OF ELEVEN YEARS AS EXPERT WITNESS IN A VERY

IMPORTANT MURDER CASE TO BE TRIED SOON THE MURDER OCCURRED

EIGHT YEARS AGO MONEY FOR EXPENSES AND A SMALL FEE AVAILABLE

YOU WOULD ONLY NEED TO COME TO NEW YORK ONE DAY IMMEDIATELY

TO EXAMINE BONES AND XXXX CONFER WITH COUNSEL AND POSSIBLY *collect*

ONE OTHER DAY *later* FOR THE TRIAL PLEASE WIRE REPLY TO ME ADDRESS

44 GRAMERCY PARK FLORENCE AND I SEND OUR BEST REGARDS

FREDERIC WERTHAM

Dr. Ashley Montague :— exhaustive
exam. confirms girl.

1220-S

WESTERN UNION

The filing time as shown in the date line on full-rate telegrams and day letters, and the time of receipt at destination as shown on all messages, is STANDARD TIME.

MAR 22 AM 6 42

Received at

NK46 137 NL=NEWYORK NY 21

MINUTES IN TRANSIT	
FULL-RATE	DAY LETTER

ATTORNEY JAMES DEMPSEY JR=
      THE COURT HOUSE

THE FORMER UNFORTUNATES ASSISTANTS OF DOCTOR GRETORY HOPE
YOU WILL MAKE FULL EXPOSURE STOP AT TIME DOCTOR GOLDWATER
INVESTIGATED HIS ACTIONS AT BELLEVUE HE WAS ASKED TO FACE
CHARGES BUT HE WAS AFRAID SO RESIGNED STOP NEWSPAPERS
PUBLISHED THAT HE WAS CRUEL DICTATORIAL AND HAD SINISTER
ALLIANCE WITH POLITICIANS STOP IN OTHER CASES SIMILAR TO
FISH HE HAS CARELESSLY DIAGNOSEDPATIENTS CONDITION AT
HOSPITAL EVEN WHEN HE HELD PATIENTS THREE TO FIVE MONTHS
FOR EXIMATIONS STOP IN COURT CASES HE TESTIFIED FOR
WHICHEVER SIDE PAYS HIM REGARDLESS OF TRUTH STOP IF TIME
PERMITS WE COULD SUPPLY YOU WITH SPECIFIC DATA ON CASES
WHERE HE STATED THE PATIENT WAS SANE AND THEN AFTERWARDS
PATIENT WAS PROVEN INSANE OR VISA VERSA STOP HE IS NOW
BEING SUED SEVERAL CASES AGAINST HIM ARE AWAITING ACTION
WILL COMMUNICATE WITH YOU FRIDAY=
      GERTNER.

211

READY TO CALL FISH SANE.

Alienists for State to Be Heard if Needed, Says Prosecutor.

Special to THE NEW YORK TIMES.

WHITE PLAINS, N. Y., March 16.—Although the State has rested its case in the trial of Albert H. Fish for the murder nearly seven years ago of Grace Budd, the prosecution is holding available alienists who are ready to testify that Fish is legally sane, District Attorney Walter A. Ferric of Westchester said today. The trial will be resumed Monday.

PEOPLE V. ALBERT H. FISH

ANTECEDENTS:

(1) **Father:** Capt. Randall Fish
    Born: Augusta, Maine, 1786
    Died: October 16, 1875 at age of 89
    Washington, D.C. 6th & B.St.N... of
    apoplexy

    (a) Father had a younger brother named Ezekiel Fish,
    who died in Augusta, Maine in 1877. Afflicted
    with religious psychosis. Committed to an institu-
    tion in Maine.

    (b) Sister- Ann - considered crazy.

    (c) Father -32d degree mason(Alma Lodge)

    (d) Left Maine and went to Philadelphia. Captain of a
    barge for Stephen Gerard for years. All children
    by his first wife born there. 5 children by first
    wife who died in Philadelphia. Lived on Teoga St.
    in Philadelphia. All children by first wife dead.

    (e) He was eight years a widower. Married second wife
    in Philadelphia prior to 1859.

    (f) First son by Ellen F. Fish, born in Philadelphia
    on Feby 1, 1859.

    (g) Came to Washington in 1860.

    (h) Lived rest of his life in Washington on B St.
    between 2 and 3d N. Leased to A.B. Cochrane farm
    towards Chevy Chase; raised hay, horses fodder,
    etc. Sold it to army (cavalry) during Civil War.

Mother:
    Maiden name: Ellen Francis Howard
  (a) Born: Perth Amboy, N.J. Dec 25, 1837

  (b) No brothers or sisters.

  (c) Died: Bright's disease, Newark, N.J.
    City Hospital Sept 11, 1903

  (e) Had left eye removed in Providence
    Hospital in Washington in 1880, by Dr.
    Mormion After that she showed mental
    symptoms. Blind in that eye since she was
    12 years old.

  (f) Showed mental symptoms; heard noises;
    saw things in street.

  (g) Went to work in Redemption Div. of Treasury
    Dept. in 1876-1885.

  (h) Also worked in Bureau of Engraving and Printing

Half Brothers(By father's first wife)

1. Leander - first born; went out West to prospect for
   gold. Buried money under tree. Came back 2 or 3 years
   later. Couldn't find tree and became raving maniac.
   Died Redwood, Cal. in an institution.

2. Hiram Born Phil. Dead

3. Ruth

4. Harriet

5. Bolton

Brothers & Sisters - by own mother.

1. Walter. Born Feb 1, 1859. Phil. Ran away from school.
   Joined U.S.Navy in Washington, D.C. in 1876. Served
   until 1881 (5 years) Honorably discharged. He is the
   one who told daft. about Cannibals, Chinese and savages
   eating human flesh. Deft then about 10 or 11. After he
   got out of navy, he got 3 months furlough with ay.
   In N.Y. He met Capt. John Davis of S.S. Tacoma;
    Walter with him about 4 years.

   Never married

   Last heard from through American Consul at Wales in
   1890. Whether dead or alive is unknown.

    Quick tempered - violent.

   Baptized: St. John's P.E. Church 16th and 8th St. N.W.
             Washington, D.C.

2. Albert Howard Fish.
   Born Washington, D.C. about 1861
   Baptized St. John's Church
   Died 18 months of age.
   Imbecile. Cause of death- water on the brain.
    This is important. Died 1862-3

3. Ruth. Born about 1863
   Died in infancy at age of 1 yr.
   Cause of death unknown

4. Harriet. Born about year or so later. Died in infancy.

5. Annie. Born Feb 1, 1865. Married Herwood Welch. Child-
   Marie. She is alive in Newark, N.J. Lived at 191 Johnson
   Ave. in Belleville, Newark, N.J. May live there now.
   Annie died newark, N.Y. in 1901. She fell apart from
   some malignant disease. She saw a peddler fall in front
   of her house in 1900. Waggon went over his head. Crushed
   his skull. She became maniac.
     On July 4, 1901 she was hanging up wash and someone
   shot her in right hand. Never got over mental affliction.

214

6. Edwin J.
Born May 2, 1868, Washington, D.C.
Heavy drinker at 17
Lost many jobs on that account
Never got along with deft. Not heard from in
15 years. Then living at 40 F. Street, N.W.
Washington, D.C.
Try to locate him or find out if dead.

7. Hamilton Fish
Born May 19, 1870
Baptized St. John P.E. Church 16th and 3th Street,
N.W. Washington. Confirmed there also
Baptized and confirmed by Rev. John Vaughn Lewis
Bishop Parett of Md.

At age of 3 deft. had St Vitus Dance
St. John's orphanage, 2'th and F Street, N.W.
Sister Sarah in charge. Learned there how to
lie, beg and steal.
Severely whipped
There 1875-1877. Had St Vitus dance while there.
Learned there to masturbate and boys got down
on him.

School: Force Bldg. 14th and K St N.W.
Market School 21st and K St N.W.
School at 5th and P St, N.W.
       "   "   7th and S Street, N.W.
From 1878 -1885 . Left at end of
8th grade.
Had St Vitus spells in chool.

First Arrest: About 1886,-1887 after deft left
school He took name of Albert H. Fish because
boys used to make fun of name. Distant cousin
to Hamilton Fish of Garrison, N.Y.
Passed worthless check on butcher named
Weaver 21st and A St, Washington, D.C.

Left Washington in 1894 and went to work at
Sanford Hall, Flushing - 165 insane people.
Worked there 2 years to 1896. Painter - saw
all kinds of cases.

Children:
1. Albert and wife Mrs Anna Straube
419 Astoria Blvd, Astoria
2. Mrs. Anna Collins, 2301 Astoria Blvd
3. Henry
4. Eugene- 2106 24th Ave, Astoria
(wife and 2 little ones)
5. Mrs Gertrude De Marco, 805 Astoria Blvd.
6. John C.C.C. Camp, Smokemount, N.C.

Married:
1. Feby 5, 1898 Holy Communion Church, 6th Ave
and 20th St -Anna May Hoffman. Still
alive- never divorced.
2. Newark, N.J. - Selma. Boy 10 yrs old
411 Hill Ave, Newark, N.J. 1930.
(lived with her about mo) (Friendship
Magazine, Medina, N.Y.)

3. Feby 5, 1930, Columbus Ohio
Mrs Myrna Nichols, Bartlett, Ohio

4. Mrs Estella Wilcox, Waterloo, Iowa, 1930

Name of
Hamilton
Fish

5 CENTS PAY NO MORE

SUNDAY MIRROR

FINAL

MUrray Hill 2-1000

Registered U. 6. Patent Office

Copyright, 1935. Daily Mirror Inc. 235 East 45th St., NEW YORK N Y

Entered as second class matter Jan. 2, 1923 at the Post Office, New York, under the act of March 3, 1879.

Vol. 4. No. 10 PR

Published Each Sunday

New York, Sunday, March 10, 1935   56 Pages Including 20 Page Magazine and Sixteen Pages Comics

MURDER MONSTER TO PLEAD INSANITY

Story on Page 3

[1936-37?]

A PSYCHIATRIC LYNCHING ?

Frederic Wertham, M.D.
New York City

ALBERT H. FISH, a house-painter, 64 years old, lured GRACE BUDD, a young ten year old girl to a lonely house. He killed her and dismembered her body. For a period of six years no trace of the murderer was found. Then, a letter was received by the mother. This letter written in incredibly cruel fashion, stated that the writer had killed her daughter and that he had cut off pieces of her flesh and eaten them. He related in the same letter other cases where a man had "stolen" two young boys, spanked and tortured them, and eaten parts of their flesh. He ended by saying that he did not violate the girl, although he easily could have, and that she died a virgin. The envelope of the letter had some printed return address on it which was imperfectly blotted out, and which led to the arrest of the murderer within a short time.

Fish, when apprehended, confessed immediately, and guided the authorities to the secluded scene of the murder and to the place where he had hidden the bones of the girl.

In his family history during the last two generations there were beside Fish himself, three psychotic persons and four severely abnormal personalities. Of the three psychoses, one paternal uncle suffered from a "religious psychosis" and died in a State Hospital; one half-brother died in a State Hospital; one brother was feeble-minded and died of hydrocephalus. Of the abnormal personalities, his mother was held to be very queer and was said to have heard things on the street and to have seen things; a paternal aunt was considered "crazy"; a brother was a chronic alcoholic; a sister had some sort of "mental affliction".

Between the ages of 5 and 7, Fish was in an orphanage. There he saw in action, a female teacher who delighted in whipping young boys on their bare backs. He received his first sexual excitation from being whipped by her and seeing others so whipped. He was a fidgity child and suffered from enuresis until the age of 11.

His sexual life was one of extraordinary abnormality. It included acts of sadism (including the infliction of severe bodily injury on minors, especially boys), masochism, active and passive flagellation, piqueur acts, sadistic defloration, homosexuality, penilinctio, cunnilingus, active and passive anilinctio, exhibitionism, voyeur acts, writing of obscene letters, fetishism, undinism, all sorts of oral and anal erotism. In addition to that, he practiced from "sexual desire" intermingled with religious-mystical ideas, active and passive coprophagia, cannibalism, and drinking of human blood, and made attempts at castration and self-castration. His sexual instinct seems to have been precociously developed and of abnormal intensity until the very end of his life.

As he grew older his sadistic and auto-sadistic activities became more and more pronounced. He beat and tortured children, forced them to do coprophagia and similar things and compelled or enticed them to force him to such identical practices. He beat himself with a nail-studded paddle which was later found. He had a consuming desire to castrate boys and made several attempts to do so. On one occasion, he cut off part of a colored boy's penis, but was overcome with fright when he saw the boy's expression, left a $10. bill on a chair beside the child and left the city. There were other similar incidents.

-2-

FISH'S WEIRD ACTS TOLD BY CHILDREN

His Devoted Daughter Weeps on Stand—Son Testifies He Professed to Be Christ.

PROSECUTION RESTS CASE

Justice Close Denies Defense Motion for a Directed Verdict of Insanity.

Fish WAS a Family Man

Back in 1923, Albert Howard Fish was a typical family man. No thought of murder crossed his warped brain as he posed for this snapshot with his daughter, Mrs. Gertrude de Marco, and his grandchild. He appears to be like millions of other men of middle age, which is exactly what makes his type dangerous

He married and had six children. One day his wife suddenly left him with another man, whereupon he continued to bring up his children faithfully and conscientiously, acting as both father and mother to them, as he expressed it. They attested to his great kindness to them at all times.

He was a house-painter, which was an occupation permitting him to indulge in his nomadic impulses, and he worked in no less than 22 different states and countless towns and cities. He frequently had to leave one locality or another after the rape of a child.

When he was about 55, a number of circumstances in his life and mentality changed. The onset of a definite psychosis can be dated back to about this time. He left his children and lived alone in a rooming house. He was arrested on two occasions for writing obscene letters to many people, letters in which he described in vilest terms the things he actually did. The report of a Probation Officer during this period quotes a statement from one of his daughters that "at times he showed signs of a mental disturbance". Twice he was sent for observation to mental hospitals. He was arrested three times for larceny and for breaking his parole. His hearing became impaired on both sides. At about this time he became more and more engrossed in religious speculations about making a human sacrifice, purging himself of iniquities and sins, atonement by physical suffering and self torture. Intensely interested in religion all his life, at this time he became more and more imbued with this subject. At times, he identified himself with God and felt he should sacrifice his own son. He began to stick needles under his finger-nails and to insert needles deep into his perineal region, 29 of which were shown by X-ray deep in his abdominal cavity, some of

-3-

them fragmented by erosion (Fig. 6). He had visions of Christ and also at times heard Christ's voice speaking to him. For example, he heard the words "stripes", "rewardeth" and "delighteth", connected them with verses from the bible, and elaborated the ideas associated with these words delusionally with his sadistic pre-occupations. He felt that he was ordained by God to castrate boys.

It was with this intention that he entered the home of the child he subsequently murdered, with the original purpose of luring her brother away. In murdering her, he felt that he "should sacrifice her in order to prevent her future outrage". In his confession to the authorities, he stated that at the time of the murder he thought she was a boy. He choked her, cut off parts of her flesh, took them home and cooked them with vegetables. Over a period of nine days he ate it. He confessed to me later that he had previously murdered a little boy under similar circumstances--one of the unsolved child murders in the New York City area.

Physically of clearly asthenic habitus, Fish's mental make-up was introverted and infantilistic. He suffered at times from seemily unmotivated "gloomy spells" lasting up to several days. He never had any feelings of love or friendship for a mature person. Whatever feelings of affection he had went to children.

He was of average intelligence, but various tests, such as the Rorschach test, indicated definite diminution of his intellectual faculties.

His pupils were slightly irregular. There was some thickening and tortuosity of the arteries of the retina. The colloidal gold curve was: 0011210000. During one examination he became quite dizzy and had to hold on to the chair to maintain his position.

-4-

* * * *

During the course of the trial, four doctors testifying for
the prosecution made, respectively, the following statements:*

Question.** Is there enough in that record for you or any other
psychiatrist to pass on the man's mental condition? Answer. Why,
surely there is, because if it had been an insane person---- Q. Now,
if you please - you say surely there is. Is that your answer, "Surely
there is"? A. Since he is not insane naturally the record is not
voluminous.

Q. You mean to say it is not necessary to find out the family background? A. Not always. If you find a man sane, that family background is alright. What his family background might be if the man is
well isn't necessary. If I am insane then my family history might
help me---but if I am not sick it is not necessary.

Q. Do you mean to tell me that you can look at a man and tell me
whether he is sane or insane or suffering from psychosis? A. Well,
sometimes, on some occasions; on other occasions one has to examine
very carefully in order to find out.

Q. How do you have a careful examination when you are really trying
to find out whether a person is mentally sick or not. A. You see,
if you find that the man shows some evidence of mental trouble, not
very definite, then you dig into everything, get all the information
you can. But there are cases that are obvious, if you look at them you
know they are insane. There are others that one examines very carefully.

Q. I am asking you how do you find out when you want to go into the
matter carefully? A. Well, if I would go to do it very carefully, you
mean detailed, I wouldn't only examine his family history, but everything
else in his life. But for the purpose of determining whether a person
at a given time is sane or insane the City only provides sufficient help
to do that practical work. If I had only one case a day it would be a
different thing. So that myself and my staff concluded after a careful
examination of this man that this man was not insane, and therefore he
was reported to the Court as not insane. Q. In otherwords, your explanation now is you didn't have an adequate staff or adequate time?
A. Well, we never had it.

----

*) Footnote: People vs. Fish. Court of Appeals, State of New York, 1935.

** Footnote: The questions asked by the lawyers are in themselves not of
   significance for this paper, which is concerned only with the assertions
   made by the doctors.

-5-

226

A. If I had to put on record every person's statements that I saw I would have to have a hundred clerks to take it down.

———————

Q. You did not take his statement down, did you? A. No, we cannot do all these things. It was a very obvious case. This man was sent to the hospital by the Court for a very trivial offense, as they call it, that he was sending obscene letters through the mail, and they wanted to know whether he was sane or insane.

———————

Q. Now, if you find a man who for mental reasons is dangerous to other people, do you commit him? A. That has nothing to do with it. If the man is sick — Q. If a man for mental reasons is dangerous to other people, do you commit him? A. Whether he is dangerous or not, I will commit him. Danger has nothing to do with the commitment of mental cases. Mental condition is sickness. As a pneumonia patient will go to a hospital, so a person suffering from a mental disease will go to a hospital. Danger has nothing to do with it. Committing a crime has nothing to do with mental diseases.

———————

Q. In your opinion shouldn't there have been an inquiry instead of being directed along the lines "Why did you send these letters?" shouldn't it have been an inquiry along these lines, "Did you do the things that you referred to in your letters?". A. No, not necessarily. It might have been a good thing to do that, but it was not necessary.

———————

Q. There are some things referring to what we have talked about in the file here as No. 1 and No. 2 (drinking urine and coprophagia). Did anybody find out or even ask the man whether he had done anything with No. 1 and No. 2? A. Why should they ask anything about that sort of thing, because that is a common sort of thing. People are arrested for writing obscene letters quite frequently. The United States Court sends these patients back and forth. Q. Is it a common sort of thing for people to have sexual abnormalities with respect to urine and human excretion? A. Well it is much commoner than you think. Q. I mean for people to drink urine and to eat excretion? A. Yes. Q. You doctors call a man like that — A. Masochistic. Q. Do you call a man who drinks urine and eats human excretion sane or insane? A. Well we don't call them mentally sick. Q. That man is perfectly all right? A. Not perfectly all right, but he is socially perfectly all right. That is, he can adjust himself to society and laws and regulations. Most of us might be abnormal here, but yet socially we are all right. Therefore, we have our liberties, and we have not come into conflict with the law. Q. In your opinion, a man sixty years of age or more who does those disgusting things knows right from wrong and knows what he is doing? A. Otherwise, yes. Q. Not otherwise. Does that man, a man who eats human excretion at sixty — A. As far as his social status is concerned, he is supposed

-6-

to be normal, because the State of New York, Mental Hygiene Department also approves of that. That is, a man of this kind cannot be sent to an insane asylum.

Q. What do you call that trouble (coprophagia)? A. That is a masochistic perversion. That is, there are people that must be humiliated in order to have sexual excitement. A man away up socially and otherwise, and financially, is sometimes unfortunate enough to have an aberration of that kind, or a sex perversion of that kind. Q. He could still suffer from that and know the difference between right and wrong? A. Of course. Not only that, they are very successful people, successful artists, successful teachers, successful financiers.*

Q. Don't you find psychiatrically that there are individuals part of whose mental make-up is retarded at the age of six months to a year while part of their mental make-up grows so that they, when they take that feces and put it in their mouth, they are then at that time acting as a child of six months or a year? A. No, no, if a child does that sort of thing it is accidental, more or less.

A. Yes, he has some kind of an aberration, some sort. That is a freak of nature, an error of nature.... Q. You are a scientist. All of these things have mental origin, do they not? You don't call a man who does those things a freak of nature. There is a mental reason for that, isn't there? A. Why, yes.

Q. Speaking about intelligence, in this particular case the intelligence of this man, according to your own reports, is about nine years; isn't that right? A. No, nothing of the sort. Q. Read that please..... What mental age is given there? A. It says here nine years and six months. There is another one.

Q. You cannot express an opinion as to whether a person is suffering from mental disease unless you have the facts, unless you have the material; that is right isn't it? A. Oh, yes, of course, my own observation and examination first, and the other facts corroborate my own observation and examination.

Q. And, as a matter of fact, at the time this man was in the hospital, about how many other patients were you examining and trying to diagnose? A. I was examining them continuously.

Q. Did you find any evidence of any needles in him? A. No.

Q. Did that fact have any significance to you, that he was praying while he was in the bath-tub down at the Hospital? A. I suppose that was the best place he could do it, because the rooms were so crowded with other patients, they were all one on top of another, and that might have been a very good place for him to pray if he wanted to pray.

---

*) At this point the counsel for the defense remarked to the Court: "Now we know what's been wrong with the stock market".

-7-

Q. Did you find many patients in the Hospital praying in the bathroom because it was the best place they could pray - is that right? A. That is no significance at all. Those are immaterial things.

Q. And paedophilia? A. Well, no, there is no definite proof of that in my opinion. Not only did he work in places where there were children also, but he worked in places and had relationship with grown up people. Most of the experiences that I got from him were in certain sanitariums where there were grown up people, so I couldn't say that he shows that definitely.

Q. Assume, doctor, that this man received in 1917, in 1922, in 1925, in 1928, and subsequently, messages, and that he saw hallucinations, would that affect your opinion one way or the other? A. If you assume those things to be absolutely the truth, I would say that it would only affect my opinion to this extent, that he may be suffering from an aggravated psychopathic state, but I don't believe that in and of itself these isolated instances occurring over such a period of time would spell out a definite insanity of any form.

Q. Now taking the assumption I just gave you about hallucinations and delusions over this period of time, and adding to that the further assumption that this man for fifty years had been practicing these sex abnormalities referred to, would that in any way indicate to you that the man was laboring under any mental disease whatsoever? A. It would not.

Q. Didn't you say that he started in, according to the statement, at seven or eight years, and then culminated by one after another, each more aggravated than the one before, until this killing? A. I would not say that they were more aggravated, one more than the other.

Q. In your opinion, in a case covering a history of approximately 50 years, do you think you can get enough information to pass a competent opinion on the case in three hours' investigation? A. Yes, sir.

A. I would hate, frankly, to be tested on the events of the last five years and have me tie them to the year in which they occurred and be accurate 50 percent or 75 per cent of the time.

Q. Assume that during that period from 1928, down to the present time, that on one occasion for a period of about a week this defendant set fires on the floor of a toilet, and that he stood there watching the fire - when asked to put them out he didn't do it, and seemed to be a little mad when finally the fires were put out, and they did so much damage during that period of time that they had to put a new floor in the room - would that indicate to you at all that the defendant was

-8-

229

suffering or laboring from any mental disturbance or disorder? A. No.
He was able to move himself so that he got the proper amount of heat
and stimulation, as far as he was concerned, but of course the floor could
not move and it probably got burned a little bit. But we have no history
that he suffered any infection or any serious injury or required medical
attention to these stimulations.

Q. Did you know that there is in evidence here that it shows they gave
him the test to take 100, and take 7 from it each time, and after he got
the 93 the first time that every other one, right down the line, was in
error. Did you know that?....that is apparently a common test? A. That
is a standard test, and it is not so easy the first time for many individuals of average intelligence.

Q. The fact that a man can speak coherently, or the fact, as you say,
that he might understand he is in a court room today---that doesn't indicate with any degree of conclusiveness whether or not he is sane or insane, does it? A. Yes, the fact that he talks coherently means there
is a certain cohesion of his personality - he is working together,
starting with the whole self - he is not divided or split up into different parts.

Q. Did you go into the question of the statement of the defendant that
at the time of the killing he thought Grace Budd was a boy? Did that
show to you any confusion of ideas? A. No. That is a very common experience in everyday life, of the changing of identity of the individual
in one's mind during the sex act.

Q. Don't you find that where you do have individuals suffering from
paranoia and afflicted with a paranoid psychosis, that it often is
with great difficulty that the alienist and the psychiatrist are able
to determine the existence of hallucinations and delusions? A. Ordin-
arily it is not difficult at all, if you make the right approach.
Q. Isn't there an effort on the part of many paranoid patients to
conceal or to fail to disclose the hallucinations? A. The paranoid
patients - that is, if I may distinguish for a moment the paranoid from
the paranoia. Paranoid individuals are usually rather frank and free
and let things out rather easily. The paranoic individual is a little
more reserved. This individual has been described to you as a paranoid
type of individual.

A. If I might say it, this individual does not have the constitution
and personality and make-up that particularly favors a paranoid reaction.

Q. Assume that because he has it there in a letter that he wrote to
Mrs. Budd, that he did that. Will you state that that man could for
nine days eat that flesh and still not have a psychosis and not have any
mental disease? A. Well, there is no accounting for taste.

Q. Do you state here that this man could take the flesh of that girl down to his room and eat it over a period of nine days and still be as sane, as defined by law? A. I think he might. It is most absurd, but we run into extraordinary things.

Q. Do you say that he could eat human feces and know what he was doing at the time, and be sane as defined by law? A. Absolutely.

Q. Isn't it a fact that sometimes that condition exists, that is, playing with the urine and feces due to the fact that part of the mind stops say at the age of six months to a year, whereas the balance of the mind functionally may develop? A. Well, it is a matter of appetite and intensive satisfaction, and the individual may do very repulsive things and still be a seer, I mean a very wise man. Q. And still be sane? A. And still be sane.

Q. Tell me how many cases in your experience you have seen of people who actually ate human feces, of your own knowledge? A. Oh, I know individuals prominent in society - one individual in particular, that we all know. Q. That actually ate human feces? A. That used it as a side dish with salad.

Q. Do you mean to say that all a psychiatrist needs to pass an opinion upon a man's sanity or insanity is, say, four or four and one-half hours of examination? A. It satisfied me in the situation. Q. Then, why is it that men are sent to Hospitals for thirty days or for three weeks? A. The law provides a limit of thirty days that they may be under observation and be studied so as to give a fuller report.

A. In paranoid states, once the fact develops they usually become enlarged upon, elaborated upon, and they are progressive. Q. And does the pattern change? A. No, it essentially remains the same.

Q. Isn't it a fact that very often people suffering under a paranoid psychosis may go on for days without giving any objective evidence of it? A. They usually reveal signs of it.

Q. It is not very hard to detect when a person has a psychosis; is that correct? A. Usually not - it may be difficult sometimes.

Q. In your experience or in your opinion would a trance or partial trance be a symptom that you would usually encounter in a paranoid psychosis? A. It is difficult for me to think of such a case.

-10-

FISH, ON TRIAL EVE, WOUNDS HIMSELF

Cuts Chest and Abdomen With Soup Bone Sharpened on Floor of His Cell.

INJURIES ARE NOT SERIOUS

State Ready to Begin Case Against Him Today for the Murder of Grace Budd

Q. Assuming for the moment that this defendant at the time that he killed Grace Budd on June 3, 1928, was operating under a divine delusion, would he in your opinion after the commission of that crime conceal it for a period of six and one-half years? A. No; he would proclaim it rather than conceal it.

_____

Q. Such a delusion or hallucination would not be confined only to what he said, is that true? A. No, he would write it and live it.

_____

Q. Assume that in one of the letters he states that the reason why he believes in flagellation, being whipped and whipping other people, is because of a reference that was had, that as Jesus was whipped and lashed so he believes that he should be - might that be an indication of a paranoid condition, associated with that sex weakness; isn't that right? A. No.

_____

Q. Where you have difficult cases with long histories, in an effort to get the full and complete facts it does take a month or six weeks? A. No, I wouldn't say that. The reason for your thirty days is that you cannot drop every other person in the community that you may have under observation and examination to do that work specifically and alone. You have to do it when you can. For that reason, you are allowed sufficient length of time that way.

_____

Q. Do you personally believe you got the full history of this defendant in two hours and a half? A. Well, If I did not I should not testify.

_____

Q. Did you find in the two hours and a half, for instance, that the defendant had set a number of fires? A. Yes, I did. Q. You have that in your record? A. Yes. Q. Have you got that in your notes? A. No, I have not. Q. The Doctor who examined the case with you testified that he did not recall that, and he looked in his notes. A. It may be that I am confusing it with the testimony during the week. Q. You have no independent recollection and you have no notes to the effect that the defendant had set fires? A. No, I have not.

_____

Q. A man might be laboring under a psychosis for years and yet only intermittently would there be symptomatic evidence of it; isn't that right? A. I have my doubt about that. Q. Sir? A. I have not seen any such cases as that of a man laboring for years under a psychosis without it being ascertained.

_____

Q. Take a man that has got a psychosis, we will say, with a psychopathic personality. Couldn't you see him on any number of occasions, and find a man so afflicted, rational - and on other occasions find that he was acting under the influence of that disease? A. Well, he might be cured, he might be well when you would see him. Q. In other words, when a man has got a psychosis or a mental disease is he always acting under the influence of that psychosis or mental disease?

-11-

234

A. He either has it or he hasn't it. He is always acting under the
influence of it. Q. But there is not always objective evidence of the
fact that he has it. A. I think so, yes. If a man has a psychosis,
there must be objective evidence of it. Q. Do you say, for instance,
that a man with a paranoid psychosis would always be acting under it
so that it would be observed at all times? A. Yes, progressive. Q.
But a man with a progressive paranoid psychosis would act under the influence of delusions and hallucinations as they came to him, wouldn't
he? A. Well, they are always present, he is living in them, they are
guiding his conduct all the time.

Q. Haven't you seen any number of cases where men mentally ill, suffering with psychosis of one form or another, and I have in mind particularly a paranoid psychosis or a psychosis with a psychopathic
personality, haven't those men later been able to tell what they did
when they were acting under that psychosis? A. In a paranoid psychosis
I am quite sure that the statement of the individual could not be relied
on as to what he did. Q. Couldn't he tell what he did? Could he relate what he did? A. I doubt it.

Q. In your opinion can a man drink urine and eat human feces and not
have a psychosis? A. He can. Q. In other words, in your opinion a
man can do those things and know at the time he is doing them what he
is doing, and not know that it is wrong; is that right, sir? A. Yes.
I had a patient who did.it. Q. Sir? A. I had a very prominent
public official who did it.

Q. I am asking you whether a man can do that (eat feces) and have no
defect of reason, and by defect of reason I mean a mental disease.
A. Yes, he can.

Q. You have known a great number of cases, have you not, where paranoid
condition existed but they were not ascertained in an examination taking
two hours and fourty-five minutes? A. I cannot say that I know a great
number of cases under any such condition.

Q. In your opinion does a man who eat human flesh know right from
wrong? A. He may, yes. Q. Assume, that this defendant took part
of the body of Grace Budd to New York and cooked it with vegetables
and ate it over a period of nine days, in your opinion did he know
right from wrong at that time? A. I think he did.

* * * * * * * *

Q. Did you talk to him at all about masochism, that is inflicting
pain on himself in order to obtain sexual pleasure? A. No. Q. You
didn't talk to him about that, did you? A. No.

Q. You did not ask him anything about that sort of thing? (dangerously
perverse acts) A. I told him that they have nothing to do with sanity

-12-

235

A. He either has it or he hasn't it. He is always acting under the
influence of it. Q. But there is not always objective evidence of the
fact that he has it. A. I think so, yes. If a man has a psychosis,
there must be objective evidence of it. Q. Do you say, for instance,
that a man with a paranoid psychosis would always be acting under it
so that it would be observed at all times? A. Yes, progressive. Q.
But a man with a progressive paranoid psychosis would act under the influence of delusions and hallucinations as they came to him, wouldn't
he? A. Well, they are always present, he is living in them, they are
guiding his conduct all the time.

Q. Haven't you seen any number of cases where men mentally ill, suffering with psychosis of one form or another, and I have in mind particularly a paranoid psychosis or a psychosis with a psychopathic
personality, haven't those men later been able to tell what they did
when they were acting under that psychosis? A. In a paranoid psychosis
I am quite sure that the statement of the individual could not be relied
on as to what he did. Q. Couldn't he tell what he did? Could he relate what he did? A. I doubt it.

Q. In your opinion can a man drink urine and eat human feces and not
have a psychosis? A. He can. Q. In other words, in your opinion a
man can do those things and know at the time he is doing them what he
is doing, and not know that it is wrong; is that right, sir? A. Yes.
I had a patient who did.it. Q. Sir? A. I had a very prominent
public official who did it.

Q. I am asking you whether a man can do that (eat feces) and have no
defect of reason, and by defect of reason I mean a mental disease.
A. Yes, he can.

Q. You have known a great number of cases, have you not, where paranoid
condition existed but they were not ascertained in an examination taking
two hours and fourty-five minutes? A. I cannot say that I know a great
number of cases under any such condition.

Q. In your opinion does a man who eat human flesh know right from
wrong? A. He may, yes. Q. Assume, that this defendant took part
of the body of Grace Budd to New York and cooked it with vegetables
and ate it over a period of nine days, in your opinion did he know
right from wrong at that time? A. I think he did.

* * * * * * * *

Q. Did you talk to him at all about masochism, that is inflicting
pain on himself in order to obtain sexual pleasure? A. No. Q. You
didn't talk to him about that, did you? A. No.

Q. You did not ask him anything about that sort of thing? (dangerously
perverse acts) A. I told him that they have nothing to do with sanity

-12-

and insanity until you find that the patient is sick mentally, and that normal people have that sort of thing, and that we simply call them psychopathic people, and they are not accepted as patients in the State Hospitals. That is the law of the State of New York.

Q. Did you ever see a man that had all of these perversions, every one of them? A. I have read of them in books.

Q. To what extent did you go into the subject of paranoia. A. Paranoia is quite an obvious disease for an experienced psychiatrist. One finds within about a half hour that the patient has paranoia. He will talk about various delusions and persecutions, this and that, and he himself is quite anxious to talk about it.

Q. Don't you know that books upon the subject of paranoia are quite to the contrary, and that as an actual matter of fact it is often difficult for an examining psychiatrist to get the patient to talk upon delusions? A. No, that is not so.

Q. Do you mean to say that when a man has delusions or hallucinations he immediately begins to talk about them? A. He talks about them, he writes about them, that is his whole life. He lives through his delusions and hallucinations continuously.

Q. You have never heard of any paranoid cases where it is difficult to find out about the paranoic condition? A. I have seen paranoics refuse to talk about their delusions because they were unfriendly to the doctor who was examining them. But never did I see a paranoic who did not talk about his delusions, particularly if the delusion was that he was being persecuted or that he was being inspired by God. They would go to the housetops and talk about it, write about it, send letters all over. Q. It might take some time, weeks and months, to find out about it; isn't that right? A. That depends entirely on the man who is examining the patient. Some of them could not find it at all, but others can find it in a few moments.

Q. In other words, you admit, do you not, that that is not an adequate report? A. In that sense, that everything has not been recorded, because we couldn't do it. It is not our fault, it is the fault of the people.

(Questioned about commitments) A. We have nothing to do with the courts.

Q. Did you find any indication, as a result of your mental examination, that the man was dangerous either to himself or to others? A. No, he was a sane person. He might have been dangerous.

-13-

237

Q. When you asked about these letters, do you recall this question:
"How did you come to write these letters to strangers? A. I can't
explain just why it was done." Do you recall that question and that answer there? A. I don't, but that is the answer that all of them give,
those who write those letters. They do not say, "I did it". Q. And
you let it go at that, and did not go any farther? A. All those who
write letters of that kind will answer in a similar way.

Q. Did this indicate anything to you: "Q. Would there have been any
possibility of your doing that ten years ago? A. No, sir." Did that
indicate to you that there was any change at all in the man's mind in
that period of ten years? A. No, I didn't pay much attention to that.
It was not necessary.

Q. Did you see anywhere in any of these letters from the jail what
might be an otherwise normal indication, the man stating in any of his
letters in that jail that he would not be in jail if he had not killed
the girl? Did you see that? A. There is no statement that he realizes
that. He knows that. But he says that he is in jail. He knows he is
in jail.

Q. Did you ask the defendant as to whether he put any more needles in
him? A. I asked him, and he said just five since the act, but I did
not ask him if he had ever done that before. At that moment I had
gained the impression, from what he was telling me, that he had only
introduced five needles, but since then I have heard that there were 29.

Q. You have seen any number of men with masochistic tendencies who were
insane? A. I know of only one case.

Q. Medically what is a pervert? A. Oh, he is an individual whose sexual
life is different from the normal person's, and who is promiscuous in
such relationships.

Q. Assume that a man takes alcohol and puts it in cotton and puts that
into his person and sets fire to it, does that indicate an aggravated
mental condition? A. That is not masochistic. He is only punishing
himself and getting sex gratification that way.

Q. What does that mean? (psychopathic personality) A. A psychopathic
personality means that the person from early childhood has been inacces-
sible at times, who is incorrigible, and who later on may or may not develop sexual abnormalities. It also means that the person substitutes
his judgment and reasoning at times for that of other people in the community.

Q. In other words, if a man practices masochism on himself to such a
point, for instance, where he puts 29 needles in his own body, some of
those for the purpose of killing himself, or sets fire to himself, in

-14-

your opinion does that man indicate evidences of a mental disease bordering upon psychosis? A. He does not. Any act of itself, either one of those, or all three together, masochism, sadism and homosexuality does not constitute a mental disease.

Q. When the act becomes dangerous to the individual, then you have indication that the masochism has reached the point of a mental disease; isn't that right? A. No, sir, not at all.

Q. Now, in your opinion can a man drink urine and eat feces and still be sane? A. Yes, it is common amongst (sic) homosexuals.

Q. Is Drs. Church & Peterson's "Mental and Nervous Diseases" an authority upon the subject? A. I don't know. The fact that a man writes a book does not mean he is an authority, so I can't tell you.

Q. Assuming that he was standing up in an orchard with his right hand upraised, at the top of a little hill, and some distance away from the nearest person, and he said five or six times "I am Christ", would that indicate to you at all that he was laboring under any delusion or hallucination? A. I don't believe that that in and of itself is sufficient to designate the act as a delusion.

A. . . . Delusions are continous and paranoid states are continuous. Paranoid conditions are those which continue and get worse and worse. Q. That is, if he imagines he is Christ today that is a fixed belief and it stays with him? A. He would go out and tell the whole world that he was Christ. Q. Oh, now, now. Hold on. Wait a minute. A. He certainly would.

Q. Isn't it a fact that very often in paranoid cases there is a tendency on the part of that paranoid subject to conceal a hallucination? A. In paranoid, no. In paranoia it may be. There are two different conditions which have been absolutely mixed up in this case so far.

Q. But there is a tendency, is there not, among all people afflicted with a paranoid psychosis to conceal rather than reveal the hallucination or the delusion? A. There is no such thing. It is sometimes difficult in true paranoia to get at the basic thing.

Q. What is the difference between paranoid and paranoia? A. In paranoid state it is where there are delusions which are more or less systemized; but in paranoia we have a definite personality, we have a person who is suffering from one set of systeized delusions, and progressively; those delusions get worse and worse, they become enlarged all the time and the person has their entire life clouded by those delusions and everything he does is clouded by the delusions, and when he writes letters the delusions sweep into it. That is a true paranoia.

-15-

Q. What are piqueur acts? A. Well, peeking, that also is in line with voyeur acts. Q. No, piqueur acts would be like sticking needles or pins into other people for sexual motives - wouldn't that be it? A. No, I don't think so.

Q. Undinism? A. I don't know what that is. I never heard of it.

A. People who are suffering from sadism, masochism, and fetishism, take those three combined, are liable to have every one of these others combined with them - and therefore in and of itself these are only off-shoots of any perversion - because when a man is sexually abnormal he is sexually abnormal and is liable to go to all extremes, particularly if he has three various types, masochism, sadism and fetishism and ex-hibitionism.

On January 16, 1936 at eleven o'clock, Albert H. Fish died in the electric chair. According to one of the witnesses, he was calm and completely self-possessed. He walked into the execution chamber, coolly looked over all the witnesses, assisted the attendants in strap-ping the apparatus on his leg, and was then hurriedly executed.

-16-

EXAMINATIONS OF ALBERT FISH

FISH KILLED 'FOR RELIGION' SAYS ALIENIST

Feby 29, 1935.

Report of Examination of ALBERT H. FISH.

I herewith beg to submit a preliminary report on
my examinations of ALBERT H. FISH made February 12th and
February 17th 1935, at the Westchester County jail.

Albert H. Fish - divorced, 65 years of age, May 19th
of American ancestry, Episcopalian church affiliations
in youth

Heredity: His father and mother were not blood
relations. They were born in Maine and New Jersey respectively. So far as can be ascertained there was no diabetes,
goiter, nor tuberculosis in the family history. The father
married twice, having five children by the first marriage
and seven by the second, the patient being of the second
group. Among his brothers and sisters, half or whole, there
were those who were eccentric or had mental trouble - especially one half brother. One brother was feeble-minded.
Many of his brothers and sisters died in infancy. He only
knew one sister. His father was short - 5'6" in height
and weighed 225 lbs. His mother was 5'11" and weighed
175 lbs.

Personal History: Patient was the youngest child.
He was born without instruments, walked and talked at the
average age, had mumps and measles, picked his nose, was
fidgety as a child, constantly wiping his face and mouth
with his hand. He wet his bed until the age of 11 - bit his
fingernails, stammered and stuttered, but did not walk in
his sleep.

At the age of 5-6 when the father died the family
was broken up and he went to an orphan's home. Here he soon
learned to masturbate and practice fellatio and attempts
at sodomy were frequent. He early masturbated with his
sister, Sarah, and fellatio was practised with her. He was
whipped excessively at the Home and grew to like it. Hitting
the buttocks caused erotic pleasure and erections. He states
he has had a sore on the penis which came on once ten days
after intercourse.

He went to public school for the age of 7-16, after
which he was apprenticed to a house painter which trade
he has followed ever since. He lived in Washington, D.C.
until the age of 24 and was married at the age of 28, his
wife being 19, having six children - four boys and two
girls - now from 36 to 21 years of age. His wife left him
in January, 1917. She was of German extraction.

As a house painter it is of moment to record that he
has worked in at least five mental hospitals - Sanford Hall,
Flushing, 1892-1896 - Whitestone - Dr. Coombs at Corona,
Dr. Lambert at Harmon, Dr. Stearns at Indianapolis, and
Dr. Kindred at River Crest. He has been fairly steadily
employed - travelled a great deal and made from $40 to $80
a week. During his work he has had several attacks of lead
colic accompanied by characteristic pains, anemia and
weakness of the hands and neuretic pains. Was never had
continuous drop wrists - but has been treated for lead
colic on several occasions.

They went to an old so-called haunted farm house. Fish cut his penis and wanted to take it with him, but the blood frightened him. He bound it up and left him. They used to beat each other on the buttocks. He wanted to eat his penis but was sick.

This was the only real cutting he did until he cut up the Budd girl.

A little later - Minnie 7-8 years old - a hot little thing - used to dance, hurdy gurdy - down in the cellar. She would masturbate him and he would kiss her vagina. Little boys at the same time - play naked in the bath tub.

The numerous affairs with boys continued. About 1928-1929 - a matrimonial paper sought out different women- all with small sums of money. Irregular perverse acts with them.

Mrs. Nichols' episode - seven children. They rode piggy back and beat him and he would be naked - both boys and girls - all perverse - masturbation and fellatio - girls of 15 and 12, boys of 10 and 8. Also Wilcox episode and much intercourse - fellatio, cunnilingus, rectal tongue work. No cruelty to the little girls.

The Budd episode - really hoped to have the boy - choked her and put knee on her chest. Then cut off her head and body above the thighs. He began by trying to rape her, but she protested and then he tried to force her.

He tasted her blood, but it made him sick at first. Had desire to eat a bit of her buttocks. Horror and raptu e- as he cut up her body - a vision of Christ came to him. By her death she would remain a Virgin. It was a sacrifice. The vision commanded him. It was all confused- like several episodes which had been like that for the past 5-6 years. He would get into a state of ecstasy, rapture, would see a vision and hear a voice. At the age of 18 he had a sun- stroke and had hallucinations at that time. They did not last long. These states of mixed ecstasy and confusion might last a few minutes, or sometimes a few days - once or twice he would be in them for almost a week-trembling with the desire to hurt and be hurt.

On one occasion he attempted to castrate himself. This was in 1929. He would lash himself with sticks, wire hair brush which would draw blood. He would have others jump on him and beat him. Both states would occur simultaneously. It was chiefly with small boys. Sometimes he would give them money as he exhibited himself - or candy.

I omit the money irregularities. Once in Sing Sing for 16 months for embezzlement. He took money to get even for false promise concerning the job offered him. First stole when he was 16 years o a e - phoney check. Mother refunded.

Also obscene filthy letters.

Neurological Examination: Save for arcus senilis, arteriosclerosis in retinal vessels, slightly sluggish reflexes, nothing anomalous.

Mental Examination : Patient is alert, well oriented, excellent detailed memory which however on repetition shows defects and contradictions - much detail elaborated and semi-Korsakoff in type.

In arithmetic tests - memory defects come out, also in school knowledge. Masselon. Differences not good. Continuous sentence fair. Drawin. Bellevue Intelligence test ah ws 9 year, 9 months. Colloidal gold test shows degeneration of some form allied to vascular syphilis (lead?)

Conclusion: Patient is a chronic sexually perverse psychopath, to an unusual degree. His sexuality is of a very infantile type - in this sense a moral imbecile - moreover he is suffering from hallucinations of sight and hearing and is delusional. He is defective mentally, arteriosclerotic, probably intensified by lead poisoning.

In my opinion he is suffering from a paranoid degenerative psychosis, is a moral imbecile and because of both mental disease and mental defect has but an insane and perverted knowledge of the nature of his acts and a similar kind of ability to distinguish right from wrong.

Respectfully submitted

(Signed) Smith Ely Jelliffe

March 12, 1935.

Mr. James Dempsey
105 South Division Street
Peekskill, N. Y.

Dear Mr. Dempsey:

In accordance with the arrangement made by you, I visited
Mr. Albert H. Fish at the Westchester County Jail, Eastview,
on March 9th, 1935, discussed with him his past and present
history, examined him neurologically and psychiatrically, and
am formulating this report for your information.

According to his statement he was born May 19, 1870 in
Washington. He completed the eighth grade in public school.
In 1875 he was placed in St. John's Orphanage in Washington
on account of the fact that his mother was engaged at work
in the Treasury Department. It was at this place that he
first learned the practice of perverted sexual acts - the
early age at which he learned these being of particular significance. These practices continued with almost constant
regularity throughout his entire life, even during the period
of his marriage and normal sexual relations. At eight years
of age his mother placed him in a home in Georgetown and at
about that time he stated he fell out of a tree, suffered a
concussion of the brain, and was unconscious for an hour or
so. He states that as a result of this accident he has had
ever since violent headaches and dizzy spells. At this time
and during the subsequent years he had mumps, chicken pox,
whooping cough, scarlet fever and measles. He left Georgetown School at fifteen years of age. At this time he performed
many perverted sexual acts with a negro boy which included whipping which he had found to be definitely productive of sexual
satisfaction when he was whipped by one of the sisters named
Sarah at the home. He also liked to be whipped and gained
great satisfaction out of the cries and groans elicited from
his victim. There were at this time and also later many experiences with the excreta which seemed to satisfy something
within himself. The experiences were so frequent and with so
many other individuals that it would be impossible to give them
in any detail. At seventeen years of age he learned his trade
of a painter and has worked at this ever since together with
doing many odd jobs. His perverted sexual relations continued

when he came here to New York on a visit.   On this visit he
went to the Eden Musee where he saw many things.   At the Eden
Musee he saw demonstrations and dissections of the genitalia,
both male and female, which impressed him greatly.   In 1894
he came to New York and obtained employment as a painter and
handyman in a number of sanitaria, and later worked in apartment houses and so forth at this trade.   During his employment
at one of these sanitaria a patient to whom he had become somewhat attached suddenly became violently crazy, was strapped to
a cot, and taken away.   The look on his face as he was taken
away impressed Fish and has remained with him ever since.   During the description of this occasion he became quite emotional,
his chin trembled, and he broke into tears, saying that he did
this whenever he thought of the look that he saw on the man's
face.   In 1929 he joined a matrimonial bureau through which he
became involved in a series of illegitimate marriages since he
was never divorced from his wife who left him.   These experiences consisted principally of writing obscene letters and
practicing all manner of sexual perversion with these women
and the members of their families.   This occupied the years
of 1929 to 1931 so far as I can tell from his statement.   He
stated that his wife left him after they had had six children
on account of the fact that he thought the family was large
enough and would not have any further relations with her.   On
account of his indecent letters which came in to the hands of
the authorities he was arrested and sent to Bellevue for observation at the end of 1930 from which hospital he was discharged with the diagnosis of "no psychosis, psychopathic
personality, sexual psychopathy".   In giving me his history
he said it was in the summer of 1930 whereas the Bellevue Hospital transcript showed that it was December 1930 and January 1931.   During his engagement as a painter following 1931
or so he would arrange things in such a way as to lure children
into cellars or rooms which he was painting and would practice
all kinds of sexual perversions with them.   He stated that he
had never had any attraction toward his own children and had
never made any advances toward them and had scarcely ever even
spanked them in punishment.   He believed that his children
never knew of these irregular relations.   In 1931 when working
in Rockaway Beach with three other employees he stated that
they had similar relations and also relations with younger
individuals.   He again began to write obscene letters on account of which he was again arrested, sent to Kings County
Hospital where he remained for a month - the record of Kings
County Hospital showing that he was admitted in August, 1931

249

Mr. James Dempsey, 3, March 12, 1935

and discharged in September 1931. The same diagnosis was made.

He described the situation concerned in the Budd case with great detail and complete frankness and apparently with no reservation whatsoever. His primary purpose was to gain control over the son of the Budd family and cut off his genitalia. This inclination apparently persisted as an obsession ever since his experience in the Eden Musee. According to his story there was apparently no premeditation in regard to the Budd daughter but that she was available and seemed then to fall in with his obsession - compulsive idea. The murder itself was followed by an attempt to drink her blood which however nauseated him, was followed by cannibalism. The obsession to drink blood and eat human food seemed to have been instilled in him as a boy from his reading of stories of Indian atrocities and also from descriptions connected with, as he said, Perry's expedition, Spanish Inquisitions, the torture of Guy Fawkes, and Quo Vadis. He stated that he did not criminally attack Grace, that her resistence excited him, but that when she relaxed it passed off. On another occasion he described a series of sexual perversions culminating in the amputation of the genitalia of a boy. He stated that he also attempted to do this to himself, but that the pair of scissors which he used was not the proper instrument.

Throughout the description of these sexual perversions there was very little to indicate any definitely psychotic trend except for the usual evidences of obsession and compulsion connected with these sexual acts. He, however, did state that he was a member of the Free Thinkers and that the idea of whipping his victims was associated in his mind with the fact that Jesus had been switched and scourged and that therefore so must we be also switched and scourged. This idea was also definitely associated in his mind in the choice of the switches which, on at least one occasion, were cut from brambles or blackberry bushes which contained the thorns. The cutting of the flesh with these thorns and the flowing of the blood provided him with an enormous sexual and emotional satisfaction. He stated that he had always been a religious man connected with the Protestant-Episcopal Church and that he had been a sexton in a number of these churches. He was baptized and confirmed. He stated that his Sunday School teacher told his mother that he had a spiritual make up for the ministry. In connection with the description of his religious experiences he stated that he had had on many occasions visions of such clarity as to entirely present the

appearance of actuality. He stated that frequently through
his life he had had visions of Christ ascending into heaven,
sitting at the table in the "Last Supper", and that these visions
would be particularly clear when he was saying grace at
tables. He also had many visions connected with the cru-
cifiction and that in all of these delusional episodes he
could see Christ's lips moving and would often hear voices
speaking to him. He stated that he had heard a voice who
told him that he should take a child and sacrifice her in
order that she should not become a harlot. During the past
six or seven years these auditory and visual hallucinations
have become more definite. He stated that "as Christ was
tortured so should he torture other little children and
even as I have been tortured and suffered, bled and died
for thee, even so thou shalt be tortured." The torturing
of children and of himself has often been in direct response
to commands to perform these acts. These commands he believed
came directly from Christ, since he would see the face, see
the lips move, and hear the words commanding him to do these
things. During the last two days, as the result of a similar
command, he had taken a bone out of a stew which he had as a
meal, and had lacerated himself across the pubis down onto
the genitalia and also across his buttocks. These scratches
were quite numerous, of quite recent occurrence, but all of
them superficial. He stated that he could think of no particular reason for these messages except the conviction that
God had something for him to do before he died. He believed
that he should go from one place to another and that he should
fulfill these visions and as an evangelist proclaim the work
of God. He stated that he was a very good speaker and that
he could sing like Sankey.

In connection with the murder of the Budd child he stated
that "a child should be sacrificed" and that "a child who was a
virgin should be taken." This thought has been in his mind
many times but the opportunity has never offered itself to
fulfill the command at that time. He believed that there was
some connection between the flesh and the blood and the symbol of the Holy Communion. When taking Grace away he had first
intended to have relations with her but on the train the idea
came and a vision from heaven which said "This is the child,
now is thy opportunity", that he could see Christ coming down
with hands outstretched and in his robes as when he ascended into
heaven. He could also see his lips move and hear the command.

Mr. James Dempsey, 5, March 12, 1935

There were many indications of a megalomania. He believed that God had something for him to do and that the work was not yet ended. He said that no one could complain of the things that had happened. He did not believe that anyone was better qualified to do this by way of language or training. He is a great reader and has travelled in twenty-three states, and has met all kinds of people from the highest to the lowest. These qualifications were recognized and held in high estime. There were also some ideas of reference in which he stated that people would notice him on the street.

When asked what kind of a plea he put in at court he said that it was entirely indifferent to him. He knew that he was charged with murder, that he did the deed, but that it was as a result of a command of God.

On physical examination the prisoner appears as a stoop shouldered elderly man appearing somewhat older than his given age. He was rather hard of hearing. He was entirely frank, unconstrained in the giving of his history and described all of the perversions and criminal acts with an air of almost complete indifference and deatchment. He presented a marked kyphosis of the thoracic region, the costal margins were flaring, the abdomen was loose and pendulous, the chest more or less barrel shaped. There were numerous superficial fresh scratches distributed over the lower abdomen, the genitalia, and the buttocks.

The equilibratory coordination was normal. There was no Romberg present. There were no signs of ataxia or any inco-ordination in either the upper or lower extremities. In performing the skilled acts, dressing and undressing, there was no evidence of any difficulty. On rising to take off his clothes he was temporarily dizzy, swaying, and had to hold on to a chair to prevent himself from staggering. The re-flexes were within normal limits although somewhat hper-active in the upper extremity and the knee jerks but rather reduced in the ankle jerks. The abdominal reflexes were active and no pathological reflexes could be elicited. Mus-cle strength and status was normal for an individual of his occupation and years. There was no definite interference with the sensory modalities and the cranial nerves showed that the visual acuity was relatively normal and that his visual fields were roughly complete. There was evidence of moderate arterial change in the blood vessels of the fundus. The pupils were three millimeters in diameter, equal, slightly irregular, central in position, and reacted somewhat better to accommoda-tion than to direct light stimulation. His hearing was poor

in his left ear, bone conduction being greater than air conduction. The other cranial nerves show no particular abnormality.
His heart was normal in size and position, rate about 80, normal
and regular in rhythm, the blood pressure was 120/70, superficial vessels were tortuous and somewhat thickened but there was
no marked sclerosis. The lungs were emphysematous.

He appeared somewhat depressed but he was quite communicative,
not secretive nor suspicious. He did not volunteer his delusions
and there was no attempt made to force these upon the examiner
until a definite attempt was made by the examiner to develop
any delusional or hallucinatory trend. His reaction was quite
free and unreserved, respectful, and friendly. He was mentally
quite alert, somewhat depressed and worried but almost entirely
detached. There was practically no real appreciation of the
significance of his act. There was no increase in ordinary
motor activity. He was quite voluble and detailed and cir-
cumstantial in his description of everything connected with
his story. In general his stream of thought was consistent,
relevent and coherent. At times he would break off one idea
and start in with another but this was not particularly evident. His content of thought showed the presence of delusional
and hallucinatory ideas together with a disturbed insight and
judgment indicating that the performance of the act had been
the result of delusional and hallucinatory auditory and visual
experiences. He was entirely oriented as to time, place, and
person. He was able to carry out simple arithmetical problems
without any hesitation whatsoever and his school knowledge of
events and so forth, also geography, was fairly well maintained.
He was able to indicate the essential differences between various kinds of animals and also between abstract ideas. In
giving his story he was able to give dates and addresses and
names connected with all of the experiences through which he
had passed with apparent ease and certainty. Certain of these
however, were found to be inaccurate and incorrect.

Except for the degenerative processes connected with this
period of life there were no evident disturbances of bodily
function. There was the indication of some general arteriosclerosis.
In his history there were two elements which may be of some
significance - the injury and unconsciousness for a period of
an hour or so when he was eight years of age, and the description of the symptoms attending what he states was a lead poisoning from which he suffered as a result of his occupation.
How much these factors can be held accountable for the present
situation is entirely problematical. The history of his sexual

Mr. James Dempsey, 7, March 12, 1935

perversions is so rich, complete, consistent and inclusive
that it would seem impossible for these to be fanciful. Their
existence is corroborated by the statements in the letters which
are on record. The delusional trend associated with exaggerated
ideas of his own importance, of his mission in life, and of the
direct visual and auditory hallucinations commanding him to
perform this and that act would give evidence of a paranoid
condition. These delusions and hallucinations were not forced
upon the examiner but were only obtained by him at the conclusion of the interview by careful questioning. There apparently was
no attempt to impress the examiner and the reproduction of the
messages gave the impression of sincerity and conviction. The
presence of these delusions and hallucinations would at once
introduce a grave doubt as to the recognition of the quality of
right or wrong, or of the responsibility for his acts during
these delusional experiences. It would be my opinion that
this individual is not only a psychopathic personality with
sexual psychopathy, but also that he is suffering from definite
paranoid ideas chiefly of a religious nature, that he is not
responsible for his acts, and that he should be confined for
the rest of his life in an institution for the criminally insane.

                    Very truly yours,

HAR:FWM   Henry Alsop Riley, M. D.

Fish Found Guilty of First-Degree Murder; Slayer of Budd Girl Is Calm at Verdict

Examining Grace Budd's dental records.

REPORT ON EXAMINATION OF ALBERT H. FISH

This report is based on my examination of Albert
H. Fish carried out at the Westchester County Jail. I saw Mr.
Fish there a number of times. Some of my examinations were
carried out alone, some in the presence of Mr. Fish's attorney,
Mr. James Dempsey, some in the presence of Dr. Jelliffe, some
in the presence of a stenographer. In the beginning, the defendant was somewhat reluctant; but he later on discussed with me
frankly the events of his life about which I questioned him.

In the defendant's family, both on the maternal
and on the paternal side, there were a number of individuals
who at one time or another were considered mentally abnormal. A
paternal uncle is said to have suffered from a "religious psychosis" for which he was confined in an institution in Maine.
A half-brother by the father's first wife was confined in an institution in California on account of a mental disorder. A
younger brother of the defendant died in infancy from a brain
disease. Another brother was a chronic alcoholic.

The outstanding feature in this defendant's life
is the extraordinary abnormality of his sexual life, which as
far as I can see is unparalleled in medical literature. It can
be characterized briefly by the statement that the defendant
has craved and practiced practically every sexual perversion
known. The dominant trait of his sex life was, as he himself

expresses it, "the desire to inflict pain— that is all that is
uppermost. I had a desire to inflict pain on others and to have
others inflict pain on me." His sexual life included/the practice of acts of sadism (including severe bodily injury to minors),
masochism, active and passive flagellation, attempts at self-
castration and castration of others, exhibitionism, voyeur acts,
piqueur acts, writing of obscene letters, pedophilia, mutual
masturbation, homosexuality,/sadistic defloration, pénélinctie,
cunnilingus, active and passive anilinctie, active and passive
coprophagia, undinism, fetishism, all sorts of anal and oral
erotism, cannibalism, attempts at drinking blood. With all this,
he had a general abnormal intensity of the sexual instinct.

         The defendant dates his sexual abnormality to early
childhood experiences. After his father's death, when the defendant was five years old, he underwent and witnessed frequent cor-
poral punishment in an orphanage, which aroused in him sexual re-
actions. From the age of about seventeen on, he had innumerable
sexual relationships with children and minors, mostly with boys
but also with girls. Frequently after one of these acts he
changed his address, moved from one part of the city to the extreme other side, or moved from city to city or from state to
state. His trade as a house painter gave him an excuse for
spending time in cellars and basements, and gave him a reason
for changing his clothes there, and putting on his painters overalls which he wore over his nude body. His trade also permitted
him to work in many different places. He admits that altogether

he
roamed about in twenty-three states, from New York to as far
west as Montana. On several occasions his employment was terminated because" things about these children came out".

In his general mental make-up, the defendant is
an introverted, infantilistic type of individual. Except for
his children, he has rarely had love or feelings of mature friendship for anybody. He spent a great deal of time daydreaming and
in such vicarious relationships as the writing of innumerable
letters to people whom he did not know. He derived great and
prolonged satisfaction from reading in newspapers any sort of
news that fitted in with his sadistic and other proclivities
(lynchings, etc.) It may be remarked here that he is in physical make-up a marked asthenic type, showing in his physical
attitudes, voice and movements certain infantilistic and feminine
traits. After his first wife left him in 1917 with the six
children on his hands, the youngest then three years old, the defendant characteristically continued to be devoted to his children; but married bigamistically three women in succession,
merely for financial advantages and for the gratification of his
abnormal sexual desires.

He seems never to have had any periods of de-
pression or elation; but for years he has had more or less cir-
cumscribed periods of unmotivated ill-humor lasting up to several

days, of which he speaks as "gloomy spells". During such periods
he would stay by himself and withdraw into himself, not talking
to anybody and imagining without any good reason that his children
did not like him.

Although his infantilistic make-up is predominantly
confined to his sexual development, it is not entirely so restricted.
This is shown by the fact that from his youth onward he has committed offenses against property, for a number of which offenses
he has been arrested and punished. Since he was sixteen. He has
committed these acts with a good deal of unconcern and with no
subsequent regret, much as a child who just wishes to take what
it wants, and does not think much about the taking.

Beginning about ten years ago, the defendant was in-
creasingly preoccupied with sadistic impulses of the most cruel
sort, that culminated in the xxx wish to castrate and mutilate.
At the same time he became more and more engrossed in religious
speculations about making a human sacrifice, purging himself of iniquities and sins, atonement by physical suffering and self-torture.
Some of his sadistic wishes he clearly recognized as coming from
"sexual desire", others were intermingled with these ideas of
pseudo-religious nature. Typical of this kind of behavior is
the fact that he stuck many needles into the lower part of his
body (verified by X-ray), which on the one hand afforded him
sexual gratification, and on the other satisfied his mystical

desire for self-torture.   It is obvious that such a confusion
permits him only a very perverted sense of right and wrong.
He saw at times visions of Christ, who moved his lips as if
speaking, and of angels. He developed the delusional idea that
God commanded him to torture himself and to make a human sacrifice. At times he heard voices saying such single words as
"stripes", "delighteth" or"rewardeth", which he connected with
biblical quotations with which he was familiar that had reference
to his instinctual preoccupations. The development of hallucinations of hearing was probably influenced by the fact that his
hearing, on both sides, became impaired about five years ago.
It is noteworthy in this connection that the probation report
at the time of his arrest in 1930 (on the charge of sending obscene matter through the mails) mentions the statement of his
daughter Mrs. Anna Collins that "At times he showed signs of a
mental disturbance."

        Such delusional thinking enters in a clearcut way
into the circumstance of the present offense. He ~~entered~~ went to the
home of the victim in the first place with the idea of abducting
the victim's brother; as the defendant expresses this: "I had
sort of an idea through Abraham offering his son Isaac as a sacrifice." Later he had visions of Christ:"I've seen his lips
move. I couldn't hear exactly, but from the forms his lips took

261

Albert H. Fish - 5

he told me that this girl would eventually be outraged and tortured and so forth, and that I should sacrifice her in order to prevent her future outrage."

During the examinations, the defendant was coherent and clear. There was evidence of some diminution of his intellectual faculties; He is awkward in handling material with which he is not familiar; although his ᵐᵉᵐᵒʳʸ memory is on the whole good, he becomes involved in inconsistencies and contradictions; he is apt to lose himself in details which are unessential to the test question asked; in the Rorschach test he sees forms very poorly. This reduction may be due to incipient organic changes in the brain, possibly also mild effects of chronic lead poisoning. The colloidal gold test of his spinal fluid, though not indicative of any specific disease, points to some organic abnormality.

In estimating this defendant's sanity, two factors have to be considered and ruled out; namely, the question of simulation and the possibility of that the facts that he relates may be pure fantasies. After careful evaluation of the data, I have come to the conclusion that neither eventuality holds in this case.

I can sum up my findings in the following conclusions: The defendant Albert H. Fish is an individual with a profound abnormality in his psychosexual development. On account of the multiplicity of and intensity of his morbid instinctual drives, and on account of the fact that they have definitely rendered him dangerous to himself and extremely dangerous to the community, his abnormal psychosexual make-up alone takes him out of the vague borderline group of psychopathic personalities and would render him a suitable case for commitment to a state hospital for the insane. On the basis of this constitutional abnormality, he developed insidiously a paranoid psychosis with delusions of a mystical, pseudo-religious nature and with hallucinatory experiences of sight and hearing. In addition, he suffers from a relatively mild intellectual disorder which is of importance only inasmuch as it increased the manifestations of his abnormal mental life by intensifying his lack of inhibitions and rational control.

In my opinion, therefore, the defendant, Albert H. Fish, is at the present time insane in the sense of the statute, and has been so since a period antedating for an indefinite time the occurrence of the present offense.

SIGNED:

Frederic Wertham, M.D.

FW/tbf

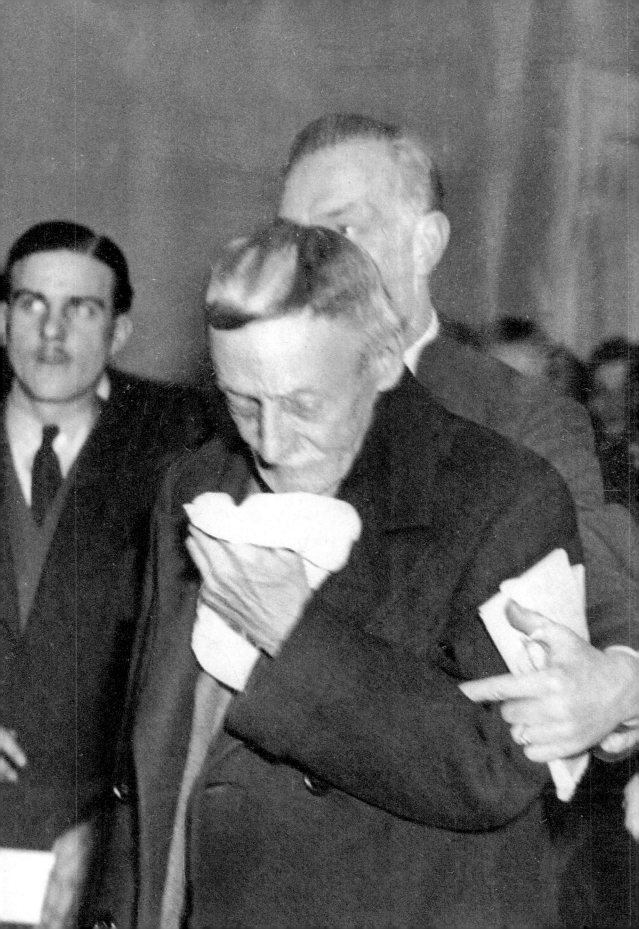

Letter written by James Dempsey, Fish's Defense Attorney.

The verdict in the case of Albert H. Fish proves nothing
else but that we are still burning witches. I believe that it was
obvious to everyone in the courtroom, including the most experienced
crime reporters in the city of New York, and to the general public,
that the aged killer of Grace Budd, who ate part of her body, is
an insane man. Anybody looking at the evidence dispassionately
must come to that conclusion, and it doesn't take an "expert" to
find that out.

Far above the question of whether this unfortunate man
should go th the electric chair or not, there is an issue here in
which the community should be vitally interested. Uncontested
evidence in the trial has shown that for many years this benighted
man has attacked, raped and tortured children. He had made no
secret of his propensities. He was arrested over and over, and
set free. *He has written innumerable obscene letters.* On two occasions he was sent by a Federal judge in
as an alleged insane person for mental observation , to Bellevue
Hospital and to Kings County Hospital. Yet the community takes
no precaution to keep such a man off the street. I believe that
in maintaining that the proper place for Mr. Fish now and a long
time ago was an institution for the insane, I am representing not
only my client, but also every citizen who has a child. Do we
have to wait until a madman like Fish commits one of the murders
that we know he has been planning in his distorted mind for almost
fifty years ? Or rather, do we have to wait until the disinte-
gration of his mind goes so far that he writes a fiendishly cruel,

obviously crazy letter to the mother of his victim, the letter
that led to his detection six years after the child's murder.
If psychiatrists who have for observation on two different occasions
a man who has butchered and eaten a little girl two years before,
have the temerity to declare that such a man is not a suitable case
for an institution for the insane, then I ask what good is this
vaunted psychiatry to anybody. If it is true that psychiatry con-
siders such a man sane, and fit to roam the streets and the cellars
and basements of our tenement houses, then as a taxpayer of the
State of New York I protest against the expenditure of/sums of money
on this socially useless ~~branch of medical~~ branch of medicine.
Suppose that through some legal technicality, say a reasonable
doubt as to the <u>corpus delicti</u>, this case had had to be dropped;
then these four our learned psychiatrists for the prosecution tell us
that the community has no safeguard, and that we have to let this
dangerous raper and torturer of children walk the street until
after a major crime is committed and tracked down.

The psychiatrists for the prosecution, one of whom had
set this man free twice, were hiding at the trial behind the most
abstruse technical psychiatric sophistries. They tell us that
there's a great difference between a psychopathic personality without psychosis and a psychosis with psychopathic personality; They
don't tell us in any understandable way what the difference between
the two is, but they openly declare their lack of social-mindedness
by stating on the witness stand that the question of whether a man
is dangerous to himself or dangerous to others "has nothing to do
with" the question of commitment ti an institution for the insane.

They tell us that the same ~~dangerous~~ diagnosis that applies to this per~~v~~erted, fiendish slayer applies to more than 25% of the general population. They admit the terrible abnormalities in this man's life and they dare to state that so shocking a symptom as coprophagia "is a common sort of thing".

They want us to believe that their hair-splitting differences between "paranoid" and "paranoia" are of any practical value to the community when it is a question of protecting it against a madman who, concededly, has violated and injured bodily more than 100 children. They tell us that praying in ~~the~~ a bathtub in the middle of the night is no indication ~~xf~~ whatever of mental abnormality, but the accepted behavior in a mental hospital; that the grossest unprintable perversions are "socially/all right" . They tell us they can just look at a man and find out whether he's sane or insane, even when he doesn't open his mouth, and that it is the accepted procedure to examine him carefully only if they have found him insane already. They tell us that if a man suffers from delusions, which I understand is the most difficult mental symptom to unravel, even for a competent psychiatrist, he lives in them and talks and writes about them all the time, so that any prison guard can know whether he suffers from them or not. These and similar statements by the prosecution alienists have driven this man to the electric chair. They are a matter of record, and will be printed in the law books when we app~~e~~al. *Some of them were cited by Justice Close in his charge to the jury*

My cross-examination of these alienists was just the questioning of a baffled layman concerning these astounding

statements, for I had always taken for f granted that a psychiatrist
first gets the symptoms and the background of the case and then de-
clares the man insane, and not vice versa. What I got in reply
were statements that people in the community who are "socially perfectly all right" have all the same unspeakable symptoms that Mr.
Fish has, and excuses about lack of stenographers, lack of assistants, lack of money. And now in an attempt to justify themselves
they stoop so low as to make the utterly false accusation that
their hospital charts must have been tampered with.

I don't believe that it requires more than common sense
to see that Mr. Fish is a diseased specimen of humanity, an insane
man. My opinion concerning xxx his mental condition is based upon
a full report submitted to me by Dr. Frederic Wertham after a most
careful and painstaking personal examination made at my request.
The facts and interpretations brought out by him xxx were confirmed in substance by the independent examinations of Dr. Smith
Ely Jelliffe and Dr. Henry Alsop Riley. The outstanding feature
in Fish's behavior is the extraordinary abnormality of his sexual
life which is unparalleled in medical literature. His dominant
trait is a mad desire to inflict pain on boys and to have them inflict it upon him. His extreme mental infantilism, the number
and quality of his morbid sexual appetites, definitely rendered
him many years ago dangerous to himself and dangerous to the community. In my opinion, this alone should take him out of that vague
group of "psychopathic" personalities which the prosecution psychiatrists made so much of, and make him x to any common sense person
a suitable mental case for commitment to a state institution for
the xinsane. But in addition to that, he developed some ten years

ago what the doctors call a paranoid psychosis, a mental disease with peculiar mystical and religious delusions and hallucinations. In his deluded brain, religious and sexual impulses xxxx became hopeleslly mixed up. Is a man sane who over a period of more than ten years inserted over 25 needles into his body in the region of his genitals, as we have verified by X-ray ? Even organically xx his brain is not perfectly normal.

Dr. Wertham was outspoken enough on the stand to state that he concluded from his intimate talks with Fish that he must have committed other xxixx cannibalistic murders. All txxx through this trial I have claimed that the prosecution, in order to put over this man's sanity, has been soft-pedalling the number and quality of his fiendish misdeeds. I now tell you that Fish is also guilty of the Gaffney murder, and that he ate special selected parts of this small boy's body just as he did of the body of Grace Budd. I shall be glad to cooperate with Detective King, who has done such splendid work in the Grace Budd case, in clearing up the Gaffney case and other murders, and I am sure Dr. Wertham will do the same.

I am appealing this case not only in justice to my unfortunate xximxx diseased client, but as a matter of public duty.

The Honorable
The Governor of the State of New York

We, the undersigned Trial Jurors, who heard all of
the testimony brought on behalf of the People of the State
of New York, and on behalf of the defendant upon the trial
of Albert H. Fish, which began on March 11th, 1935 and
terminated with a verdict of "Guilty of murder in the first
degree" on March 22nd, 1935, do hereby respectfully petition
Your Excellency for Executive clemency on behalf of this
defendant.

The defendant, Albert H. Fish, who is now
approximately sixty-six years of age, has, for many years,
been afflicted with mental aberrations and was at the time
of the commission of the offense and is today a marked
psychopath, who, according to the testimony of eminent
psychiatrists possesses certain mental diseases, known as
psychosis with psychopathic personality, paranoid psychosis
and organic brain deterioration. These expert opinions
were substantiated by a number of lay witnesses, who attested
to the hallucinatory and delusional tendencies of the
defendant and also to the complex indications of paradoxical
and perverted practices that undoubtedly raise a serious
doubt as to the defendant's sanity both at the time of the
commission of the alleged crime and at the present time.

While it is our frank opinion that the defendant
should never again be permitted to obtain his liberty, we,
nevertheless, feel that his present mental condition is such
that he should not be executed; and we earnestly request
that you exercise the discretion imposed in you as the
Chief Executive of this State, by having his sentence
commuted so that he might be confined in the Dannemora
State Hospital for the Insane or in the New York State
Hospital for the Insane at Mattewan.

We urge that such action be taken by you in the
conviction that such confinement for the few remaining
years of this defendant's life will expiate the offenses
which he has committed, as well as society can expect a
mentally afflicted man to atone for his depredations.
Furthermore, our citizens should be protected in the future
to the extent that such maniacs as Albert H. Fish be
recognized and committed before the perpetration of their
outrages, rather than by inflicting extreme penalties
after the damage has been irreparably consummated. To such
end an intensive study of Albert H. Fish by competent
psychiatrists may be of great benefit in precluding the
possibility of similar attacks by others.

While we are respectively mindful of our duty and
have earnestly performed it according to our oaths and
consciences, we are constrained to intercede for clemency
for this defendant, not only because of his mental condition,
but because of his advanced years and the great sorrow

which will be inflicted upon his innocent children and grandchildren, if the law exacts the extreme penalty of death:

William M. Foster Juror 12.

Tillmann   Juror #5.

Thomas Madden Juror No. 13

I join in this petition in requesting that an examination be made of this man's mental condition and if he is found to be insane, that he be confined in the appropriate institution

Louis S. Hirsch Juror #9

John C. Becker Juror 2

Joseph J. Garland Juror 6

John Pastabird Jury

I join in this petition in requesting that an examination be made of this man's mental condition, and if he is found to be insane, that he be confined to the appropriate institution.

James LeShim #10

Harry. J. Cooper
                    Juror. 3

George L. Burkley Juror #11

        Martin Crump Juror 4

I have no objection to Executive
clemency Henry C. Lee Jr #7

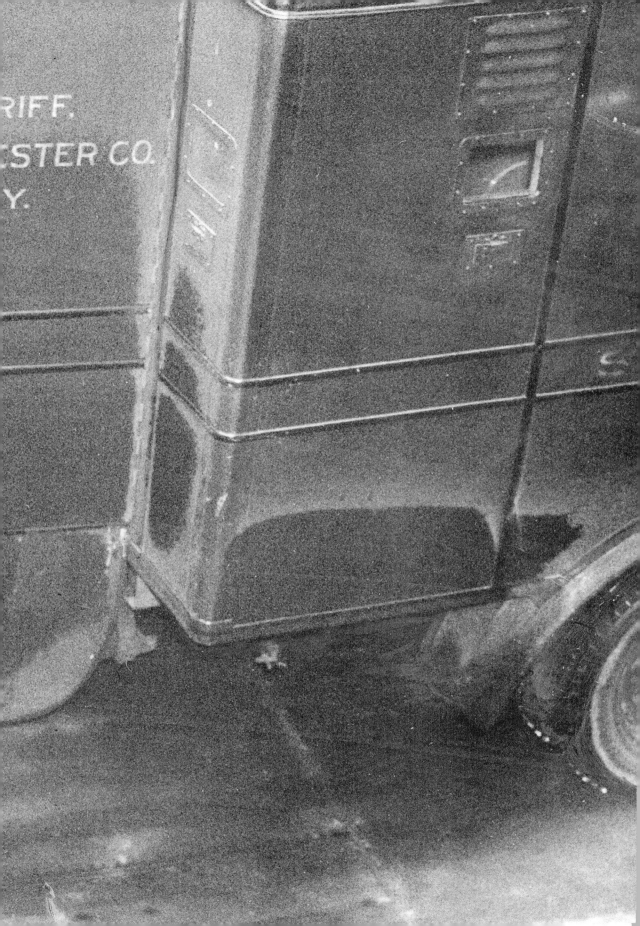

JAMES DEMPSEY, JR.
ROBERT E. DEMPSEY

TELEPHONES
PEEKSKILL 1010-1011

JAMES DEMPSEY
COUNSELLOR AT LAW
105 SOUTH DIVISION STREET
(FLAT-IRON BUILDING)

PEEKSKILL. N. Y. April 9, 1935.

Dr. Frederic E. Wertham,
44 Gramercy Park N.
New York City.

Dear Dr. Wertham: Re: <u>People v. Fish</u>

I am most grateful for your cordial and complimentary
letter of the 1st inst.   While you and I were both intensely interested in the outcome of the case, in order
that the high standards of justice might be reached in
dealing with an obviously insane defendant, the verdict
is not surprising from divers reports which I have received to the effect that some of the jurors had previously made statements that "sane or insane Fish should
be sent to the chair," and also from conversations which
I had with them after the verdict, which reveal to me that
they all rather felt Fish was insane, but that he would be
better off in another world.

It was delightful to have had the many occasions to confer with you and to prepare our defense. Your assistance
to me was invaluable, and your testimony on the trial has
brought great honor and distinction to you. I have heard
many expressions of commendation and respect regarding your
testimony.

I have still several defense objectives in behalf of my
client:

    1. I am preparing the case on appeal, and I will
give you a copy thereof when it is printed. The appeal will
undoubtedly be heard before the Court of Appeals in Albany
during June or October terms of the Court. There are many
errors in the record, in my opinion, and I will be surprised
if the Court of Appeals affirms the verdict. However, if they
do, my next step is,-

    2. To make application to have another mental examin-
ation of the defendant in Sing Sing. He shows now noticeable
signs of the terrific strain: his hands are shaking, and he
is trembling all over. The principal keeper, Sheehey, told
me that he has torn up sheets of linen and mattresses, so
that they have him sleeping on bare "ticks". When they went
to bathe Fish last Saturday they found marks upon his body
which had been put there several days previous thereto, and
which had been self-inflicted by means of a sharpened bone. Now
they have him constantly under guard for twenty-four hours a day,

F.E.W. 2

and every few hours they strip him naked and search him.
It would be fine if you could see Fish some day at the death
house at Sing Sing.

3.   Coincidental with the mental examination at Sing
Sing, I intend to personally see the jurors in the case, to
have them sign a petition requesting executive clemency for
Fish upon the grounds of his insanity. While I do not think
I can get all of the twelve jurors to sign such a petition,
I believe that I will get more than half. Armed with such a
petition, and with the other data which I have regarding
Fish's mentality, I will then appeal to the Governor to
have his sentence commuted to life imprisonment, and to have
him committed to a state institution for the criminal insane.

Altogether, I am firmly of the opinion that Fish will never
come to his end in the electric chair, for henceforth we
will be pleading his case before men of superior learning
and erudition.

No doubt you have read the minutes of the trial (or most of
them). I will appreciate your reaction and suggestions for
incorporation in the brief which I am writing.

We have been victorious, at least, in the larger court of
public opinion.

I must prepare affidavits to be signed by you and Drs. Riley
and Jelliffe as to the dates when you testified and the
dates when you saw the defendant and the time that you devoted to conferences with me. Please advise me in this regard, setting forth the great number of hours which you devoted to this case.   Upon receipt thereof, I will prepare
an affidavit, and either deliver it to you personally, or
forward it to you for execution by you.

Enclosed herein is a letter which I received some days ago
from San Diego addressed to you, which I had intended
to give to you personally.

With kindest regards to Mrs. Wertham and yourself, I am,

                              Cordially yours,

JDJR/B
(Encl.)

277

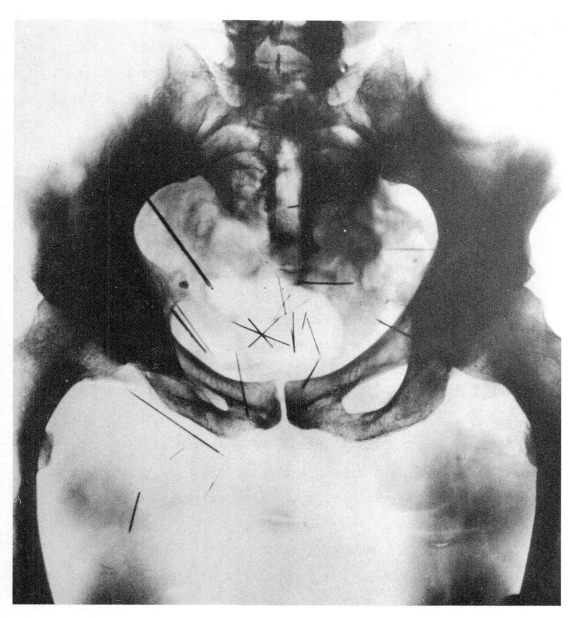

X-Ray of Fish's abdomen showing needles.

The Court. Albert H. Fish, in accordance with the law the sentence is that you be delivered to the custody of the warden of the State Prison known as Sing Sing in Ossining, New York, there to be confined and to be put to death, according to the manner provided by law, during the week beginning April 29, 1935.

State of New York
County of Westchester SS.

To the Agent and Warden of Sing Sing State Prison at Ossining, in the County of Westchester and State of New York, situated in the Ninth Judicial District of the State of New York, in the Criminal Branch thereof, held in and for the County of Westchester, at the Court House at White Plains in said County on the 22nd day of March 1935, Albert H. Fish, was duly convicted of murder in the First Degree for having murdered Grace Budd, in an indictment mentioned, by the verdict of a jury.

And the said Albert H. Fish, having been arraigned for sentence on the day and date hereof, upon said conviction and judgment;

NOW, IT IS HEREBY ORDERED AND ADJUDGED on the motion of Hon. Walter A. Ferris, District Attorney, that the said Albert H. Fish, be and he hereby is sentenced to be executed according to the laws of the State of New York; and

IT IS HEREBY ORDERED that the execution of the said sentence be made upon him, the said Albert H. Fish, upon some day within the week beginning the week of April 29th, 1935, by causing to pass through the body of the said Albert H. Fish a currant of electricity of sufficient intensity to cause death, and the application of such currant to be continued until said Albert H. Fish is dead. Said execution to take place within the walls, yard or enclosure adjourning or within the State Prison at Ossining, West-

Prison.

IN WITNESS WHEREOF, I Frederick P. Close, a Justice of the Supreme Court of the State of New York, in and for the Ninth Judicial Department, and the presiding Justice at said Court at the time of the arraigning of the said Albert H. Fish, on the date thereof, have given this our warrant under our hand and the seal this 25th day of March 1935.

Frederick P. Close
Justice of the Supreme Court.

Bernard A. Koch
    CLERK.

(seal)

I HEREBY CERTIFY that the defendant above named was examined, on oath, by the Court, before Judgment was pronounced; he stated that his true name was Albert H. Fish, that he is of the age of 64 years; that he was born in Washington, D.C.; that he is married; occupation painter; that he has been in Prison or Penitentiary before; yes. Grand larceny 2nd, 12-9-03, sentenced 13 months to 3 yrs. 3-8-06, returned to Sing Sing Prison, violation of parole.

(seal)

BERNARD A. KOCH
    CLERK.

Sing Sing Prison

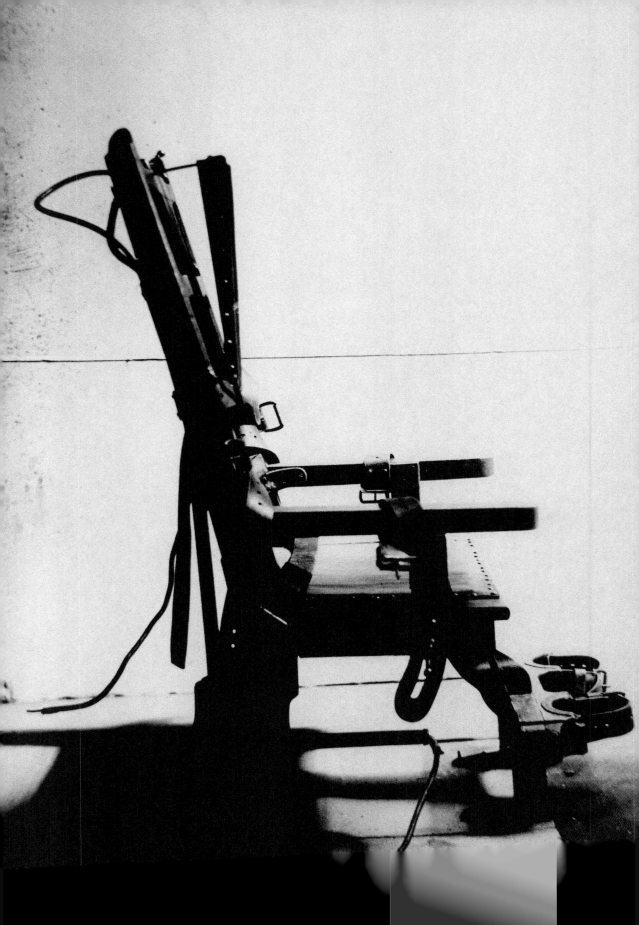

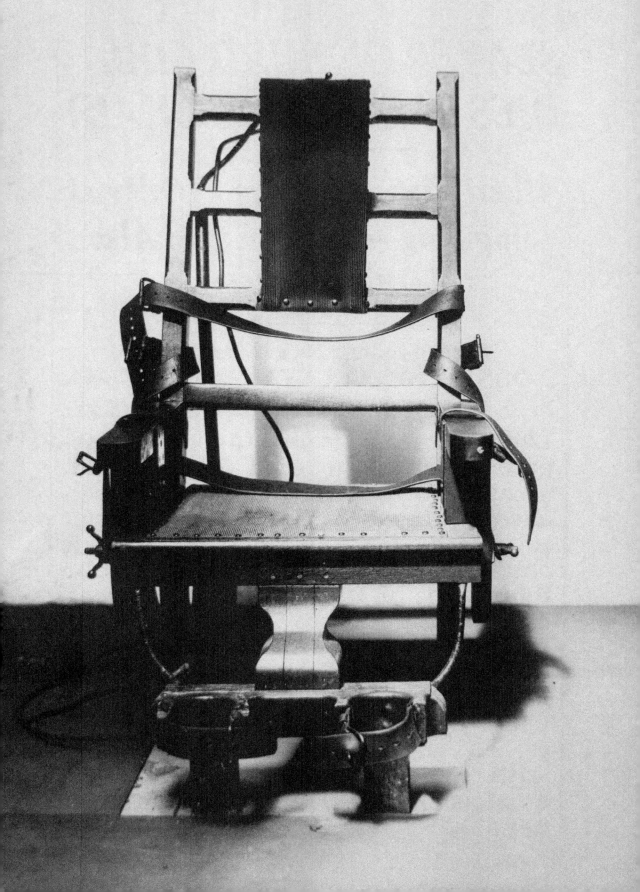

SLAYER OF BUDD GIRL DIES IN ELECTRIC CHAIR

Albert Fish, 65, Pays Penalty at Sing Sing—Bronx Negro Also Is Put to Death.

Special to THE NEW YORK TIMES.

OSSINING, N. Y., Jan. 16.—Albert Fish, 65 years old, of 55 East 128th Street, Manhattan, a housepainter who murdered Grace Budd, 6, after attacking her in a Westchester farmhouse in 1928, was put to death tonight in the electric chair at Sing Sing prison. John Smith, 41, of 203 West 144th Street, Manhattan, Negro restaurant proprietor, who was convicted of killing James Wilson in a fight in the Bronx, preceded Fish in the chair by a few minutes.

Fish entered the death chamber with his hands clasped in prayer at 11:06 P. M. He was pronounced dead at 11:09.

"there was the aged killer of a little girl in New York who had stuck pins and needles in his body because he enjoyed the sensation. Speculation was rife as to what might happen when the current coursed through him. Some expected to see sparks fly in all directions, but nothing unusual happened"

FROM *AGENT OF DEATH*
THE MEMOIRS OF AN EXECUTIONER
BY ROBERT G. ELLIOTT
NEW YORK • E. P. DUTTON & CO., INC. • 1940
Mr. Elliott was Fish's executioner at Sing Sing Prison.

PART V: CORRESPONDENCE

**Confesses Three Slayings;
Two Nearly 25 Years Ago**

KING FEATURES SYNDICATE
235 EAST 45TH STREET
NEW YORK 17, N.Y.

Wednesday [6 May 1970]

Dr. Wertham:

I'm in the midst of turning out a
book for Lyle Stuart, the publisher, on the Albert
Fish case of the early Thirties, and of course
I've read with great interest your comments on the
case in your superb "The Show of Violence."

I plan, naturally, to discuss your
role in the trial and I wonder if you think it
would be worthwhile for me to come visit you and
talk about it, or whether most of what you might
have to say is in your book?

Any suggestions, help or comment
will be appreciated.

Sincerely,

Mel Heimer

MLH:BS   Mel Heimer

BLUEHILLS
Kempton R#1
Pa. 19529

May 8, 1970

Mr. Mel Heimer
King Features Syndicate
235 East 45th Street
New York, N.Y. 10022

Dear Mr. Heimer;

I always like to help a writer if I
can and shall be glad to be of any
assistance. Yes, there is more to
be said about the Fish case in its
ramifications and meanings and con-
firmation of what I wrote in THE SHOW
OF VIOLENCE.

There have been a number of very
wrong things said and written about
it and you may also want to ask me
some questions about that. I have
made some comments about the Fish case
in A SIGN FOR CAIN (Paperback Library
1969) on pp. 223 and 226.

Unfortunately I am at present exceed-
ingly busy, so I would suggest that
we talk about it on the phone. The
best time to call me is Sat.or Sun.
or Mon. a.m. at this Pa. number:
215-756-3496.

Sincerely,

FREDRIC WERTHAM, M.D.

292

May 25, 1970

Mr/ Mel Heimer
King Features Syndicate
235 East 45
New York, N.Y. 10017

Dear Mr. Heimer:

Enclosed some of thr reprints I mentioned to you
on the phone. And I found the list of perversions
practiced by Fish and submitted to the Court. I
have never given that out before. Herewith a
photostat of the actual list submitted at the time.

Sincerely,

Fredric Wertham, M.D.

FW/enc

293

Channing A. Corbin   204 Montclair Drive, Cheyenne, Wyoming 82001, (307) 634-6429

22 July, 1975

Mr. Fredric Wertham, M.D.
Route 1
Kempton, Pa. 19529

Front Page Detective 19 March 1975
shelf (above) books

Dear Dr. Wertham:

I called long distance this morning to ascertain your
correct mailing address. The lady who answered the
call very graciously asked if I wanted to talk with you.
I do very much want to talk with you but I thought it
would be best if I waited until you had had the opportunity
to receive and evaluate my letter.

For the past eight months I have been very dilligently
researching a classical crime case for the purpose of
authoring a book length manuscript confined exclusively
to the one subject and the one crime involved.

I have reference to the Albert Howard Fish - Grace Budd
case in which you played such a prominent role.

To digress but for a moment, I am a retired police officer.
My background has provided me with some invaluable assets
as concerns research. I enjoy striving for absolute authent-
icity and accuracy. I pride myself on an absolute and
meticulous approach.

In this instance and as an example; In the letter which
Mr. Fish wrote and mailed to Mrs Budd, among other things he
mentioned a steamer named the Tacoma and he elaborated to
state that a friend of his had sailed on this vessel to Hong
Kong in 1894. Mr. Fish described a severe famine in China
at that time and related that his friend found children being
sold for their flesh.

Interestingly enough, via correspondence with the San Fransisco
Maritime Museum and the Tacoma, Washington Museum, I have learned
that there actually was a ship named the Tacoma plying the Pacific

The National Writers Club
Crime Writer's Association (Eng.)

294

in that particular era and that the Tacoma did indeed sail
for Hong Kong in 1894. Additional research is currently
being conducted in a quest for the vessel's logs, manifests,
etc. I am curious to learn if any member of the ship's crew
was named Fish.

I have employed a genealogist as well as a researcher living
in Washington, D.C. to assist in tracing Mr. Fish's lineage
and his ancestry.

One of Mr. Fish's sons testified at the trial that his father
had told him at one time that his real name was Hamilton Howard
Fish and that he had assumed the name of a deceased brother in
early life. These tid-bits of information tend to indicate
that Albert Howard Fish AKA Hamilton Howard Fish stems directly
from the former secretary-of-state, Hamilton Fish - 1808-1893,
family. Micro-filmed census reports taken in Washington, D.C.
will be used to resolve this facet of the inquiry inasmuch as
that city did not commence the recording of vital statistics,
ie., birth certificates until 1871, one year after Albert Fish
was born.

I cite the above illustrations primarily to stress the fact that
I am in quest of authentic and factualy information only and that
it is for this purpose that I have undertaken to correspond with
you.

I am in possession of a book published in 1971 titled "The
Cannibal". Personally, I found so many inconsistancies in this
text, ie., age of the victim is incorrect, date of the crime is
incorrect plus entirely too much unfounded, sheer sensationalism
that I disqualify it as a valid source of reference. I have
several other texts which mention the case briefly and both
include a photograph of a house which is identified as being
"Wisteria Cottage". I have purchased fourteen 8X11 B&W photos
from UPI and AP to include an authenticated picture of the

crime scene and I can say with a high degree of positive
conviction that the photos published in these two books are
not those of "Wisteria Cottage". ("A pictorial History of
Crime - 1840 to the present by Julian Symons, page 238 and
Crimes and Punishment, a pictorial encyclopedia of aberrant
behavior, Vol. 17, pages 100 and 101")

I find also that numerous and uncorroborated statements and
conclusions relevant to this case have been picked up by
various writers and carried forward, perpetuated, as it were,
in the guise of factuality.

For example, "Bloodletters and Badmen" by Jay Robert Nash, pages
195 through 199 is replete with errors which seem to have been
carried on in that Nash used Mel Heimer's text, "The Cannibals"
as reference materiel.

Doctor Wertham, I would sincerely like to solicit your indulgence
and cooperation in this matter and entirely on your terms. I
look to you as an authority of unimpeachable integrity on the
subject matter.

I have your text "The Show of Violence" in my crime library
and know you to be an excellent author of considerable reknown.
I spent quite a few years in the Criminal Investigation Division
of the U.S. Army's Provost Marshal Corp and your views were
frequently cited at the criminal investigation school located
at Fort Gordon, Georgia.

I certainly didn't intend to allow this missive to run to three
or more pages and my apologies.

In conclusion, I have written Supreme Court Justice Gallagher,
Mr. James Dempsey, attorney requesting their cooperation. I
have the trial transcript, the record of appeal from Albany, NY
and all newspaper clippings from the White Plains "Daily Reporter"

and the "New York Times". I have filed letters of inquiry
with The New York Historical Society, The New York Public
Library, The Library of Congress and many other potential
sources, only to insure that I have access only to the facts
of the case and also to enable me to strip away the cheap
and sordid sensationalism that was most likely interjected
by the news media and the tabaloids of that bygone era.

My literary agent is Mr. Daniel P. King, a man who specializes
in true fact crime writings.

Sir, I will look forward to hearing from you at your earliest
convenience. At that time and if you would be so kind as to
advise me as to a suitable time that I might call you for a
more personal chat, I will appreciate it.

I sincerely hope that this letter finds you in the best of
health and thank the lady who answered the telephone this
morning for her courtesy.

Very cordially,

Channing A. Corbin

The answers to the questions, as set forth below, will
factually clarify and elucidate points of interest which
are presently somewhat vague and hazy.

1.   Do you feel that FISH killed more then once? He was
accused of involvement in other slayings. He was identified
as having been near the scenes of other crimes (Gaffney case).
He even confessed to other slayings. This factor may have
been prompted by his desire to escape the penalty.

2.   Are you firmly convinced that FISH did indulge in the
practice of cannibalism and that he consumed the flesh of
Grace Budd with sexual connotations? I ask this because it
is evident that our only proof at this late date as well as
back in the year 1935 is Mr. FISH's spoken word. Is it not
possible that his vivid and morbid fantasies were, to him -
so real that in his own mind they became FACT?

3.   Which statement do you feel is most factual; That FISH
was imbued with depravity and perversions from early childhood
OR that something within his mind snapped with the loss of his
wife Anna to another man. And a third possibility presents
itself-A combination of both?

4.   You spent a total of about 12 hours in close, intimate
conversation with Mr. FISH, in three seperate sessions. What
means did you employ to obtain his confidence at the outset?
Did he confide in you because he was able to realize that you
wanted to be helpful or was this his one opportunity to unburden his conscience totally to another?

298

5. Do you have any opinions as to why Mrs Anna FISH, wife of the defendent, was not called to testify in court?

6. I myself marvel at the unmitigated loyalty displayed by five of Mr. FISH's six children subsequent to his arrest and throughout the trial. It would seem that the siblings felt a sufficiently high degree of parental devotion to offset natural feelings of revulsion as the sordid revealations of his past began to unfold. Did this strike you as being somewhat extraordinary under the circumstances?

7. To the best of your knowledge; did Mr. FISH ever own or drive an automobile?

BLUEHILLS
Kempton R#1, Pa. 19529
(215) 756-8059

August 4, 1973

Channing A. Corbin
204 Montclair Drive
Cheyenne, Wyoming 82001

Dear Mr. Corbin:

Thanks for your letter. I shall be glad to talk with
you on the phone if I can be of any help. The best
time to get me is at about ten a.m. any morning.

My impression was that most of the things that Fish
told me were true. He made no attempt to mislead me
or to defend himself. To the best of my knowledge he
was related to the former secretary of state; but I
did no special research on that.

I am in full agreement with you about the unreliability
and sensationalism of the book THE CANNIBAL. Many of
the author's "facts" are not so.

The Fish case is very important in my opinion. It
foreshadowed the violence, individual and collective,
that has happened since and is still happening. The
conditions which permitted him to continue his murderous
career have not improved -- indeed are much worse now.
I mention the Fish case again in my book A SIGN FOR CAIN,
An Exploration of Human Violence (Macmillan, 1966 and
Warner Paperback Library, 1969 & 1973).

For some reason I did not mention in my testimony nor
in THE SHOW OF VIOLENCE that Fish was very interested
in reading about particularly cruel murder cases. Now,
following my researches on mass media influence, on
violence, I think that this is important. For example,
I recall he told me in detail about the H.H.Holmes case.
That was a particularly cruel and long-undetected mass
murder case around the turn of the century. I don't
know where Fish read about it, but if you are interested
you can read about it in John Bartlow Martin's "The
Master of the Murder Castle, A Classic of Chicago Crime",
Harper's Magazine Dec. 1943, which was reprinted in THE
PORTABLE MURDER BOOK edited by Joseph Henry Jackson,
Viking Press, N.Y. 1945.

With best regards,
Sincerely,

Fredric Wertham, M.D.   FW/eno

Channing A. Corbin

BLUEHILLS, Kempton R#1, Pa. 19529

August 15, 1975

Mr. Channing A. Corbin
204 Montcalir Drive
Cheyenne, Wyoming 82001

Dear Mr. Corbin:

Thank you for your letter and the Front Page Detective Magazine with your interesting piece. I am returning your check; it was not necessary to send it.

I have not looked at the Fish record for a long time. I would have liked then, as you say, to enlarge on my testimony. But the many interruptions interfered.

I am enclosing a reprint of another article of mine in which the Fish case is mentioned, correcting an entirely false presentation of the case.

As for your questionnaire:

1) I am convinced that Fish killed many more children -- at least fifteen. That was one of the reasons why in my plea for clemency I asked Governor Lehman to start an investigation of the whole problem. Fish made no point of how many children he had killed and in all of my contact with him he showed no "desire to escape the penalty".

2) I am sure that he ate parts of the flesh of Grace Budd. He was not given to making up fantasies. He acted.

3) I have no doubt that Fish suffered from a mental disorder. I think different factors interacted to cause his behavior.

4) I believe Fish confided in me because he realized that I was genuinely interested. He had no wish "to unburden his conscience".

5) I don't know why Anne Fish was not called to testify.

6) Fish's children were so loyal to him because, believe it or not, he was a good father to them. Despite his poverty he did everything he could to help them.

7) I never heard of Fish's owning a car and do not believe he ever did.

I wish you good luck with your work.

Sincerely,

Fredric Wertham, M.D.

FW/enc { his $25 check
        Zilboorg
        no photo (about time of hapiness) in overcoat

301

Albert Fish by Fred Burkhart

BIBLIOGRAPHY

Fredric Wertham Papers, Manuscript Division, Library of Congress, Washington, D.C.

Wertham, Fredric. The Show of Violence. New York: Doubleday & Co., 1949

King, Brian. Lustmord: Bloat, 1996

Elliott, Robert G. AGENT OF DEATH: THE MEMOIRS OF AN EXECUTIONER. New York: E. P. Dutton & Co., Inc., 1940

Victims Were All Children

By ARTHUR MEFFORD.

Positively identified as the "old man always making inquiries about little girls" in the vicinity of the crime, Albert Howard Fish, confessed thrill-killer of Grace Budd, last night was being quizzed by Brooklyn detectives concerning the murder of four little girls and attacks upon five others in that borough, within a period of less than two yeasr.

All of the victims were strangled even as the aged Ogre of Wisteria House choked to death with his withered hands, the hapless, 10-year-old Budd child.

Printed in Great Britain
by Amazon

22202004R00176